150 KNITTED TRIMS

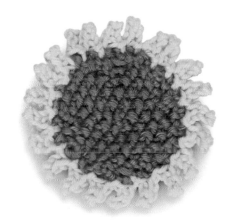

150 KNITTED TRIMS

Designs for interesting edgings, from lacy trims to
appliqués, braids, and fringes

Lesley Stanfield

St. Martin's Griffin
New York

www.stmartins.com

Library of Congress Cataloging-in-Publication Data Available
Upon Request

ISBN-10: 0-312-36325-7
ISBN-13: 978-0-312-36325-3

QUAR: KNE

First published in the United States by St. Martin's Griffin

Conceived, designed, and produced by
Quarto Publishing plc
The Old Brewery
6 Blundell Street
London N7 9BH

Senior Editor: Liz Dalby
Art Editor: Jacqueline Palmer
Managing Art Editor: Anna Plucinska
Assistant Art Director: Caroline Guest
Photographer (projects): Nicki Dowey
Photographers (directory and technical section):
Paul Forrester, Phil Wilkins
Illustrator: Coral Mula
Pattern Checker: Susan Horan
Proofreader: Ilona Jasiewicz

Art Director: Moira Clinch
Publisher: Paul Carslake

Manufactured by Pica Digital
Printed by SNP Leefung Printers Ltd

First U.S. Edition: October 2007

10 9 8 7 6 5 4 3 2 1

CONTENTS

AUTHOR'S FOREWORD

Have fun knitting trims of every kind to add to hand-knits or ready-mades. Personalize the simplest clothing or transform home furnishings. When the right trimmings can't be found you can make your own. You can create original presents and even decorate the gift wrap.

The character of your knitting will depend very much on the yarn you use. It's astonishing how different these trims can look when they're made in other yarns and colors. So experiment with yarn and needle size to find out how the finished trim will behave. Bear in mind the compatibility of your yarn with the fabric it's going to be attached to. Treat the designs in this book as suggestions and be adventurous with your experiments.

Lesley Stanfield

ABOUT THIS BOOK

The book contains a stunning visual directory of over 150 knitted trims. Once you've chosen the trim you'd like to make, use the handy trim reference number to locate the instructions for making it in the Technical Data chapter. In the Projects chapter you will discover six inspirational project ideas for using and applying the trims. The Refresher Course at the start of the book contains most basic information and knitting techniques needed to work the trims in the book; all techniques are clearly explained with step-by-step instructions and illustrations.

REFRESHER COURSE

The Refresher Course guides you step-by-step through the necessary knitting basics, from basic stitches to working textured stitches and three-dimensional motifs.

SECTION 1: DIRECTORY OF TRIMS

The Directory of Trims is a visual showcase of 150 knitted trims and is organized into seven categories: easy pieces, braids, frills and flounces, lacy edgings, loops and fringes, insertions, and additions. Each trim is shown at actual size—just flip through and pick your trim.

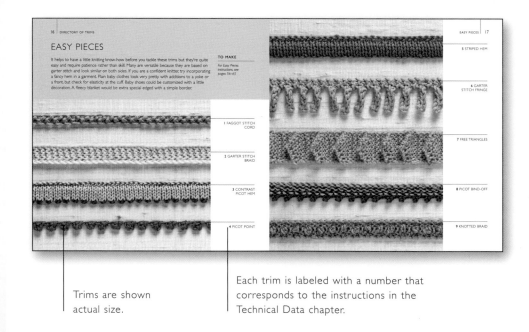

Trims are shown actual size.

Each trim is labeled with a number that corresponds to the instructions in the Technical Data chapter.

SECTION 2: TECHNICAL DATA

Here, you'll find the patterns for every single trim along with information on the yarns, beads, and sequins used to make them. There is also a detailed photograph of each trim, going in closer than the directory so that you can see the stitches in detail. The Technical Data section is also organized into the seven trim categories and each trim is labeled with its number as well as a page reference telling you where it is in the directory.

SECTION 3: PROJECTS

There are six attractive and inspirational items ranging from a handbag embellished with a rose motif to a funky sunhat with a textured band. All of the projects are designed to encourage you to try using the trims in the book and to experiment with varying colors and textures.

Instructions for each trim appear in full.

Every set of instructions is rated according to skill level: easy, intermediate, or complex.

Use the trim number to refer back to the actual-size photograph in the directory.

PROJECT 4: FLORAL BAG

Instructions list the trim or trims used and give advice on how to attach them.

Each project is illustrated with an inspirational picture of the finished item.

UNDERSTANDING THE SYMBOLS

The instructions for each trim are accompanied by one or two symbols indicating the materials needed for the trim and a little extra information about making and using it.

Yarn used

Beads or sequins used

Extra information

YARNS, NEEDLES, AND ABBREVIATIONS

These trims require the minimum of materials and specialist equipment.
For most of them, all you need is a ball of yarn and a pair of needles.

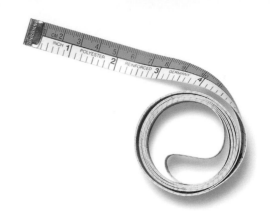

YARNS

There is a huge range of yarns available to use for knitting, from very fine cotton to chunky wool. Yarns can be made from one fiber or combine several. Smooth yarns show up stitch patterns particularly well, but do also experiment with novelty textured yarns for different effects.

Woolen yarns and blended yarns with a high proportion of wool feel good to knit with as they have a certain amount of stretch. Yarns made from hair, such as mohair and alpaca, lack elasticity but have a characteristic silky quality. Yarns made from cotton and linen are durable and may be blended with other fibers to add softness. Yarns made wholly from synthetic fibers, such as acrylic, are usually less expensive to buy but lack elasticity and cannot be blocked. A good solution is to choose a yarn with a small proportion of synthetic fibers combined with a natural fiber. The construction of a yarn will also affect its behavior and characteristics.

Yarn is sold by weight, rather than by length, although the packaging of many yarns includes the length per ball as additional information.

YARN TYPES AND WEIGHTS

Yarns are available in great variety from very fine to very bulky. The generic names given to different weights of yarn vary around the world and can therefore be confusing. For example, the Shetland yarn called 2 ply Jumper Weight is literally two strands of wool plied together but it is roughly equivalent in gauge to a UK 4 ply or a US Sportweight.

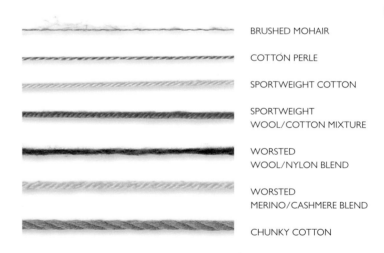

BRUSHED MOHAIR

COTTON PERLE

SPORTWEIGHT COTTON

SPORTWEIGHT WOOL/COTTON MIXTURE

WORSTED WOOL/NYLON BLEND

WORSTED MERINO/CASHMERE BLEND

CHUNKY COTTON

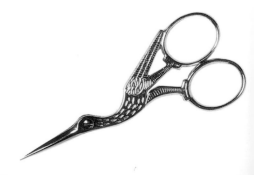

NEEDLES

For the trims in this book you'll need knitting needles in a range of sizes and a cable needle for cable stitch patterns. You may also find useful: a tape measure and calculator for working out the length of trims, scissors, crochet hooks, long quilting pins, and a tapestry or wool needle.

Pairs of knitting needles are made in a variety of lengths ranging from 10 in (25 cm) to 16 in (40cm). Most are aluminum, although larger-size needles are made of plastic to reduce their weight. Bamboo needles and circular needles are a flexible alternative.

STRAIGHT AND CRANKED CABLE NEEDLES

PAIRS OF KNITTING NEEDLES IN VARIOUS MATERIALS

DOUBLE-POINTED KNITTING NEEDLES

ROW COUNTERS

ABBREVIATIONS

Frequently-used abbreviated knitting terms are listed below and any unusual abbreviations are given with the instructions for the project. Abbreviations that might be confused—such as sk2po and s2kpo—are also explained with the relevant instructions.

k knit

kfb k in front and back of st to make 2 sts from one

m 1 make a st: lift strand in front of next st and k in back of it

m 1 p make a st: lift strand in front of next st and p in back of it

p purl

pfb purl in front and back of st to make 2 sts from one

rep repeat

RS right side

skpo slip one st knitwise, k 1, pass slipped st over

sk2po slip one st knitwise, k 2 tog, pass slipped st over

s2kpo slip 2 sts as if to k 2 tog, k 1, pass slipped sts over

sl slip

st-st stockinette stitch

st(s) stitch(es)

tbl through the back of the loop(s)

tog together

WS wrong side

yo yarn over: yarn forward under needle, then over needle to make a st

Square brackets work instructions in square brackets the number of times stated

Round brackets these are used to group stitches together

* An asterisk marks the point from which instructions are to be repeated

REFRESHER COURSE

This section highlights unusual techniques used for some trims and contains a few essentials, but it is assumed that the reader has basic knitting skills. Remember that yarns vary, so always experiment before starting a project.

MAKING A SLIP KNOT

A slip knot makes a secure first stitch on the needle.

1 Keeping the ball on the right, coil the ball end of the yarn over the other end and hold this loop in your left hand. Insert the needle into the loop from right to left, catch the ball end, and pull it through the loop.

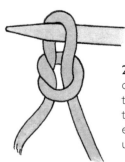

2 Pull both ends of yarn to tighten the knot and then pull the ball end to move it up to the needle.

CASTING ON

The thumb method of cast-on is recommended for the start of all projects as it gives a firm but elastic edge. Further into the project other types of cast-on may be required and these are also described here.

THUMB CAST-ON

Leaving an end approximately three times the width of the cast-on required, put a slip knot on one needle. This will be the first stitch.

1 * Needle in the right hand, hold the yarn in the left hand and catch it with your left thumb, then insert the needle in the front strand of this loop.

2 Take the yarn from the ball around the needle and make a knit stitch by pulling the needle through and slipping the loop off your thumb.

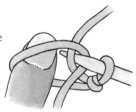

3 Pull the end of the yarn to tension the stitch and then repeat from *.

KNITTED CAST-ON

This simple two-needle method is useful when stitches need to be added to those already on the left-hand needle.

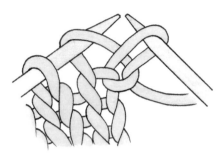

1 * Knit in the first stitch but do not slip it off the needle.

2 Transfer the new stitch from the right-hand to left-hand needle. Knitting into the new stitch each time, repeat from *.

CABLE CAST-ON

Very similar to the knitted cast-on, this gives a firmer edge. * Knit in the first stitch and transfer the new stitch to the left-hand needle, as in illustrations 1 and 2 above. Knitting into the space between the new stitch and the next, repeat from *.

HOW TO CALCULATE MULTIPLES OF STITCHES

Edgings made widthways require a little planning to estimate the number of stitches needed. For these edgings, the number of stitches to cast on is given as a "multiple of xx sts plus x." The "multiple" is the number of stitches in one pattern repeat and the "plus" completes the pattern at the end, or ends, of the row. For example, four repeats of an edging given as "a multiple of 8 sts plus 3" would be $4 \times 8 + 3 = 35$ sts.

BINDING OFF

In all these projects a simple knit-stitch bind-off is used, unless stated otherwise. Knit two stitches. * With the left-hand needle, lift the first stitch over the second. Knit the next stitch to make two stitches, then repeat from *.

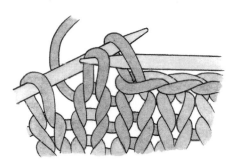

FASTENING OFF

When one stitch is left on the needle, break the yarn, draw it through the stitch, and pull it tight.

SLIP STITCHES

In these projects all stitches are slipped knitwise, unless stated otherwise. Knitwise: the right-hand needle inserted in the front of the stitch as if to knit one and then the stitch is slipped off the left-hand needle without being knitted.

LOOP STITCH

Most of the loop stitches used in these trims are made on the right side. Knit in the next stitch without dropping it off the needle, bring the yarn forward between stitches, around your left thumb and to the back. The method of then making the two stitches into one depends on whether the loop will be cut (as in Cut Pile, see page 44) or whether it will be left uncut (as in Loops and Sequins, see page 44).

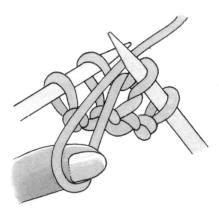

YARN OVER

Taking the yarn over the needle (abbreviated as yo) makes a stitch, either forming a decorative hole below the stitch mid-row or forming a loop at the beginning of a row. Bring the yarn forward under the needle and then take it over to be in position to make the next stitch. If this is a purl stitch bring the yarn to the front again.

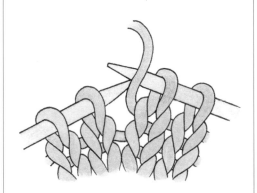

SEAMS

Mattress stitch produces an almost invisible seam. With right sides facing and starting at the cast-on, take the needle under the strand between the first and second stitches of one edge and then do the same at the other edge. Continue working into alternate edges, tensioning the stitches to close up the seam.

KNOTTING A FRINGE

The easiest way to fringe a knitted edge is to knot tassels along it.

1 Use a convenient gauge to cut strands of a suitable length.

2 Insert a crochet hook in the wrong side of the knitted edge. Fold the required number of strands for a tassel and catch the fold with the hook.

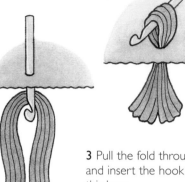

3 Pull the fold through and insert the hook into this loop.

4 Pull the strands through the loop and pull the ends to tighten the knot. Trim.

BINDING A TASSEL

Suspended tassels need to be bound carefully for a neat finish.

1 Cut strands as above, fold the required number for a tassel and tie at the top. With one end of the binding yarn, make a loop and hold this against the tassel.

2 With the remainder, bind over the loop for the required number of wraps, then thread the end through the loop. Pull the first end so that the loop draws the second end up behind the wraps. Trim both ends close to the binding.

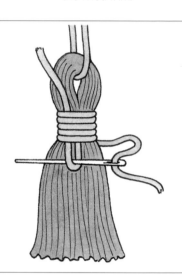

MAKING A POMPOM

Using two rings of card or plastic is probably the best-known method of making regular, round pompoms.

1 Place one ring on top of the other and use a wool needle to wind yarn around both.

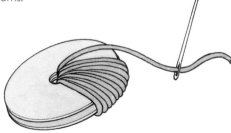

2 Starting new yarn at the outside edge, continue until the rings are tightly covered. Inserting the scissors between the rings, cut the yarn around the edge.

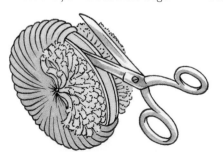

3 Take yarn for the tie between the rings, knot it tightly, and slip the rings off. Trim.

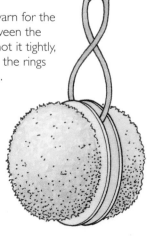

MAKING TWISTED CORD

Twisting yarn and then doubling it on itself produces a useful cord. The cord can be a loop worked into the knitting (as in Cord Fringe, see page 42) or made separately to attach a decoration (as in Pompom Fringe, see page 45).

1 Knot a length of yarn to make a loop that is slightly more than twice the length of cord required. Insert a cable needle in the loop at one end and secure the other end. Turn the needle until the yarn is tightly twisted.

2 Hold the twist taut at the halfway point and fold it so that both ends meet. Let go the fold and the cord will twist on itself.

MAKING KNITTED CORD

A more substantial cord can be made by knitting with two double-pointed needles.

Cast on three stitches and knit one row in the usual way. * Without turning, slide the stitches to the opposite end of the needle. Take the yarn across the wrong side from left to right and knit one row. Repeat from *, taking the yarn across quite firmly each time.

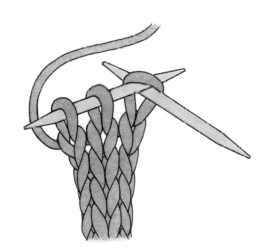

MAKING A KNITTED CHAIN

A chain resembling a crochet chain can be made very simply. Put a slip knot on the needle. * Knit one stitch, then transfer this stitch from the right-hand to the left-hand needle. Repeat from *.

THREADING BEADS AND SEQUINS

If the yarn is fine enough, threading can be done directly.

To thread a needle with knitting yarn double the end and push the loop through the eye.

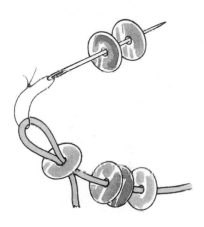

To put beads and sequins onto thicker yarn, use strong sewing thread as a carrier. Thread a sewing needle and knot the thread to make a loop. With the knot to one side, take the knitting yarn through the loop and slide the beads or sequins along the needle, loop of thread, and knitting yarn.

DIRECTORY OF TRIMS

Most of us have something to which we'd like to add a personal touch: clothing
bought impulsively; an old favorite that needs a new lease of life, or maybe a plain
piece of knitting or crochet that would be beautifully complemented with a trim.
Explore this stunning visual directory of 150 knitted edgings, fringes, braids, motifs,
and accessories and you're sure to find the trim to suit you. Each beautifully
photographed trim is displayed in actual size and labeled with a trim number that
corresponds to its instructions in the Technical Data chapter (pages 54–113), so
that once you've chosen your trim you can flip directly to the instructions.

EASY PIECES

It helps to have a little knitting know-how before you tackle these trims but they're quite easy and require patience rather than skill. Many are versatile because they are based on garter stitch and look similar on both sides. If you are a confident knitter, try incorporating a fancy hem in a garment. Plain baby clothes look very pretty with additions to a yoke or a front, but check for elasticity at the cuff. Baby shoes could be customized with a little decoration. A fleecy blanket would be extra special edged with a simple border.

TO MAKE

For Easy Pieces instructions, see pages 56–65

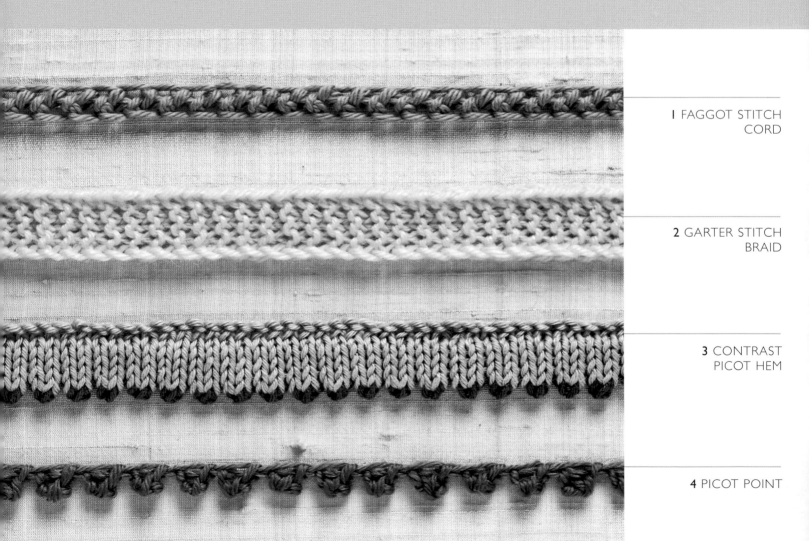

1 FAGGOT STITCH CORD

2 GARTER STITCH BRAID

3 CONTRAST PICOT HEM

4 PICOT POINT

5 STRIPED HEM

6 GARTER
STITCH FRINGE

7 FREE TRIANGLES

8 PICOT BIND-OFF

9 KNOTTED BRAID

10 BASIC LACE

11 POINTS

12 BABY TEETH

13 TAGS

14 PICOT SELVEDGE

15 CURLY FRINGE

16 OPEN PICOT

17 SAW TOOTH

18 BUTTON BAND

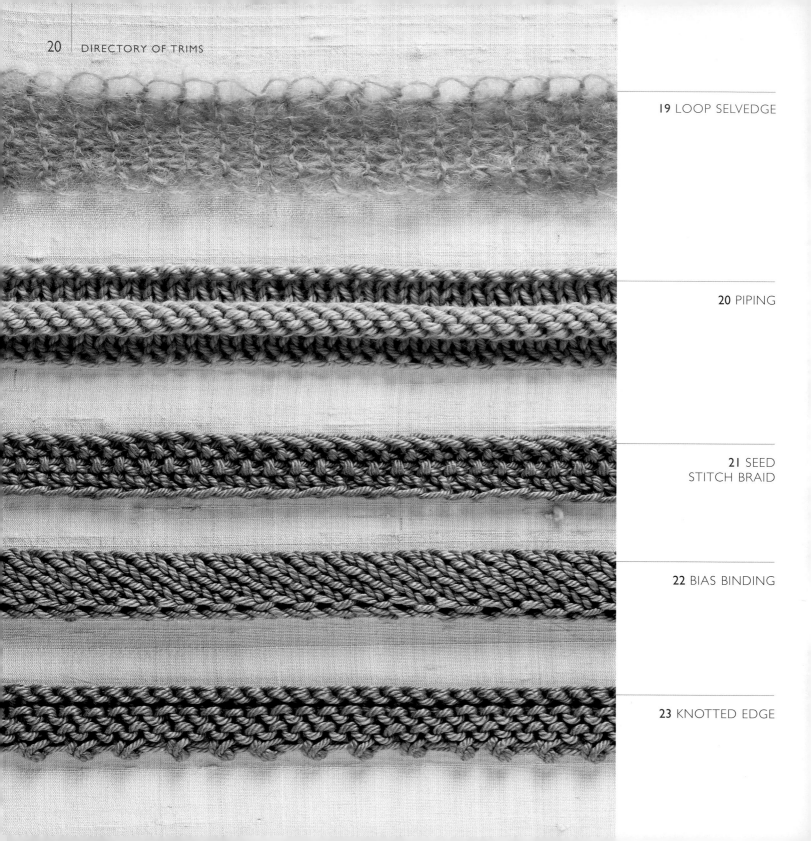

19 LOOP SELVEDGE

20 PIPING

21 SEED STITCH BRAID

22 BIAS BINDING

23 KNOTTED EDGE

24 BEADED
CAST-ON

25 BEADED
LOOP EDGING

26 NARROW
BEADED BRAID

27 WIDE
BEADED BRAID

28 BIRD'S EYE

BRAIDS

Manufacture your own braid to look like a by-the-yard product or use a single pattern repeat of a familiar textured stitch to make a braid of any colour and width. The result can be used like ribbon to neaten an edge, as a tape to cover a join or as appliqué decoration. Try weighting the edge of a knitted throw with a matching braid. Use contrasting colors to cover the seams of strip patchwork or join different braids to create a patchwork.

TO MAKE

For Braids instructions, see pages 66–73

29 ZIGZAG RIB

30 SMALL CHAIN

31 LAMBS' TAILS

32 ROPE

33 BOBBLE
AND RIB

34 WIDE BRAID

35 CARTRIDGE
BELT

36 CLUSTERED
BEADS

37 STRIPED
BIAS BRAID

38 SEQUIN BRAID

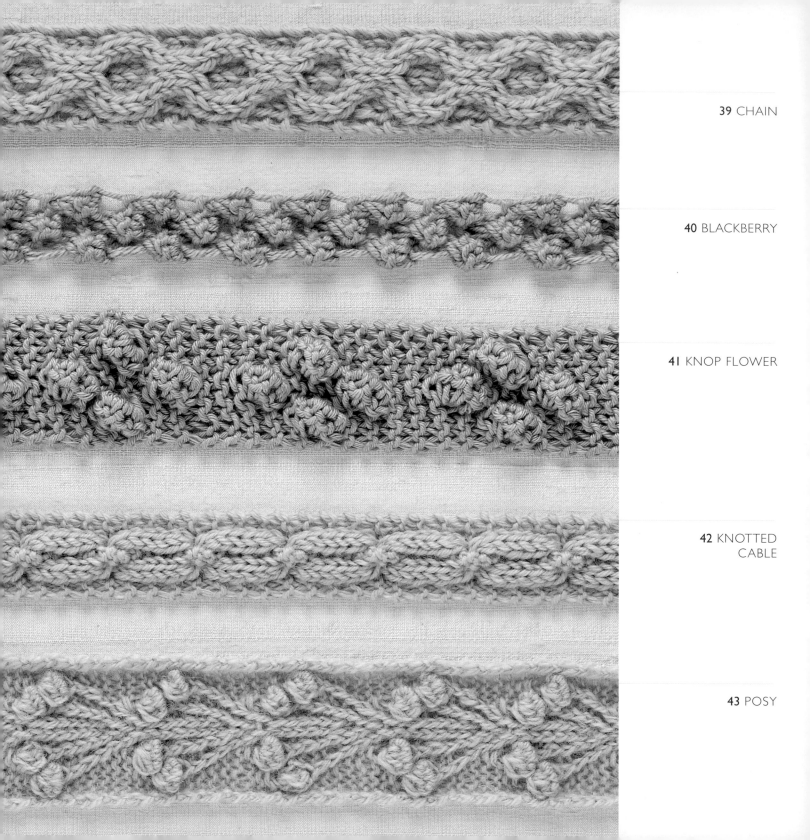

39 CHAIN

40 BLACKBERRY

41 KNOP FLOWER

42 KNOTTED
CABLE

43 POSY

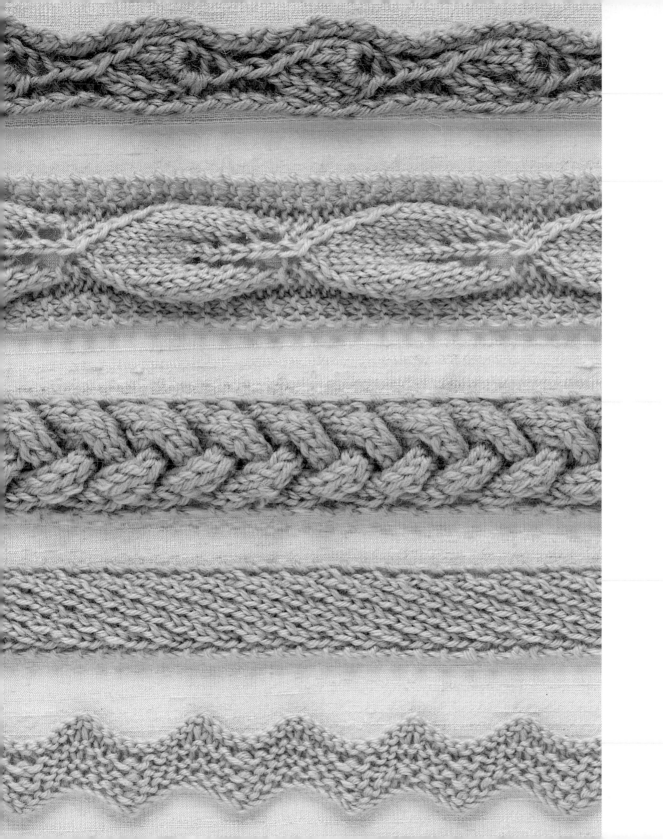

44 BUD AND
STEM

45 BAY LEAF

46 EMBOSSED
BRAID

47 TWILL

48 RICKRACK

FRILLS AND FLOUNCES

Curved, ruffled, and pleated edgings can be simple or elaborate, fine or chunky, but they always look very pretty. Some are knitted lengthwise with turning rows producing fullness, while others need more planning as they are made widthwise with decreases gathering in the stitches. Lots of fullness makes a frill that's easy to curve around a neck as a collar or ruffle. A frill will weight an edge or even flute it and can be used to turn gloves into gauntlets or a bedspread into an heirloom.

TO MAKE

For Frills and Flounces instructions, see pages 74–81

49 WAVES

50 SCALLOPS

51 BOX PLEATS

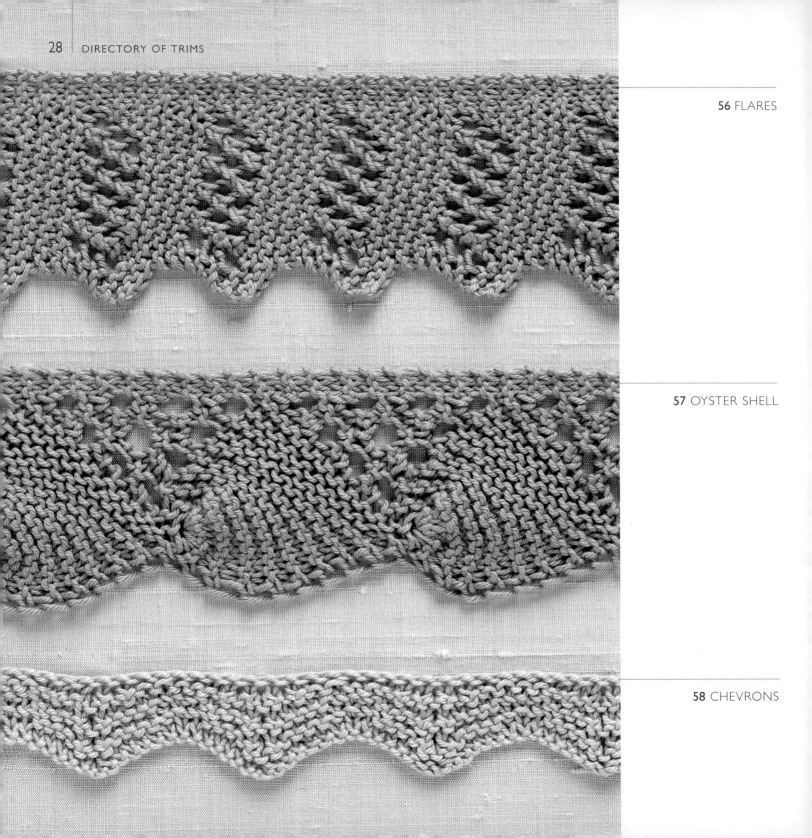

56 FLARES

57 OYSTER SHELL

58 CHEVRONS

59 HOOPS

60 FAGGOT AND
RIB FLOUNCE

61 WELTED
FLOUNCE

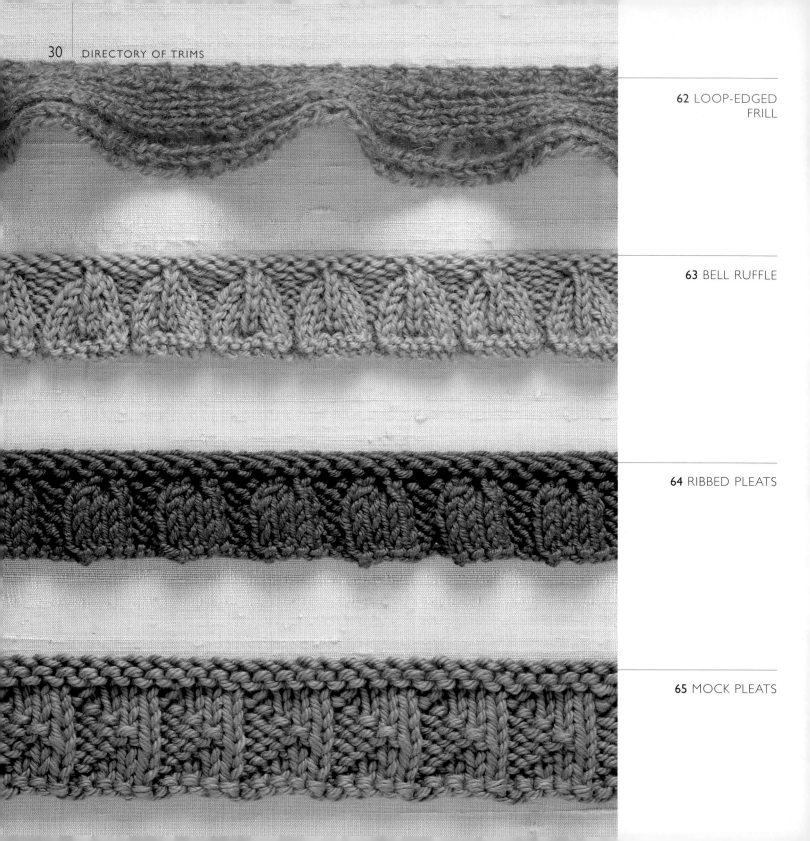

62 LOOP-EDGED
FRILL

63 BELL RUFFLE

64 RIBBED PLEATS

65 MOCK PLEATS

66 LADDER FRILL

67 WELTED RUFFLE

68 FEATHER
AND FAN

LACY EDGINGS

Lace can be nostalgic or up-to-date. Many lace stitches are based on garter stitch which gives them stability and makes them relatively easy. Most lacy "holes" are based on a yarn-over increase balanced by a decrease, so simple lace stitches are achievable and elaborate patterns are often just permutations. Experiment with yarns—plump yarns tend to blur definition unless pressed. Consider adding a lacy scallop to a scarf. Try coiling a short length of tooth-edge lace into a flower. Almost any style of lace edging could form a hat band.

TO MAKE

For Lacy Edgings instructions, see pages 82–91

69 BUNTING

70 MINI LACE

71 SHORELINE

72 ZIGZAG

73 TREFOIL

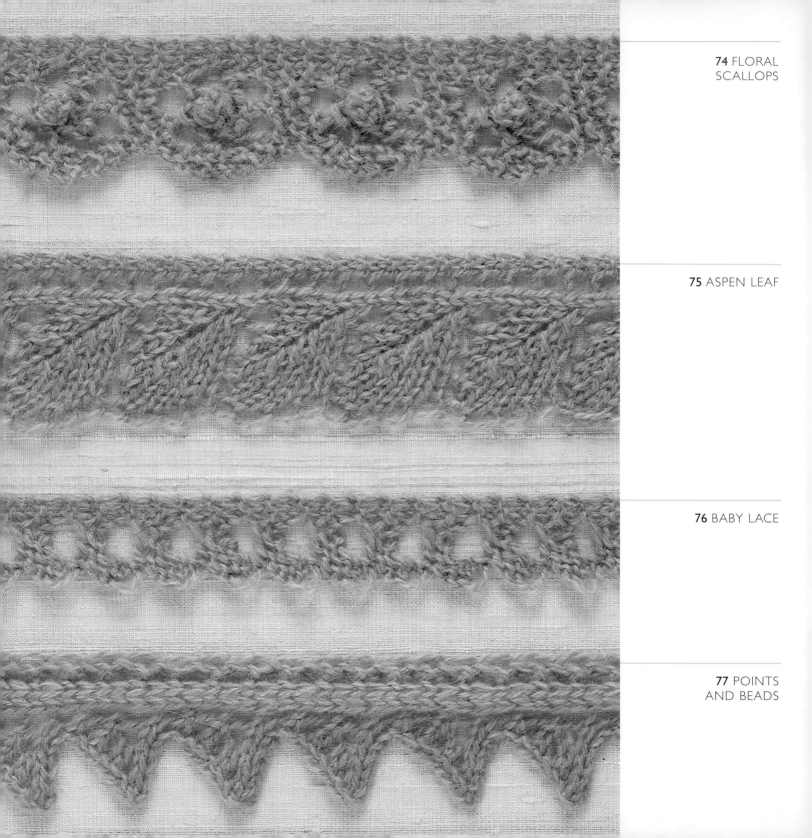

74 FLORAL
SCALLOPS

75 ASPEN LEAF

76 BABY LACE

77 POINTS
AND BEADS

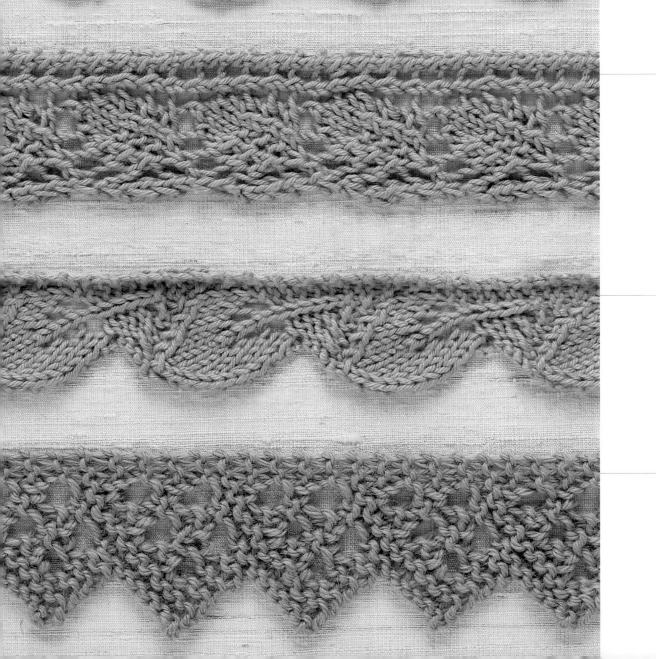

78 TRELLIS

79 LIME LEAF

80 FALLING LEAF

81 CINQUEFOIL

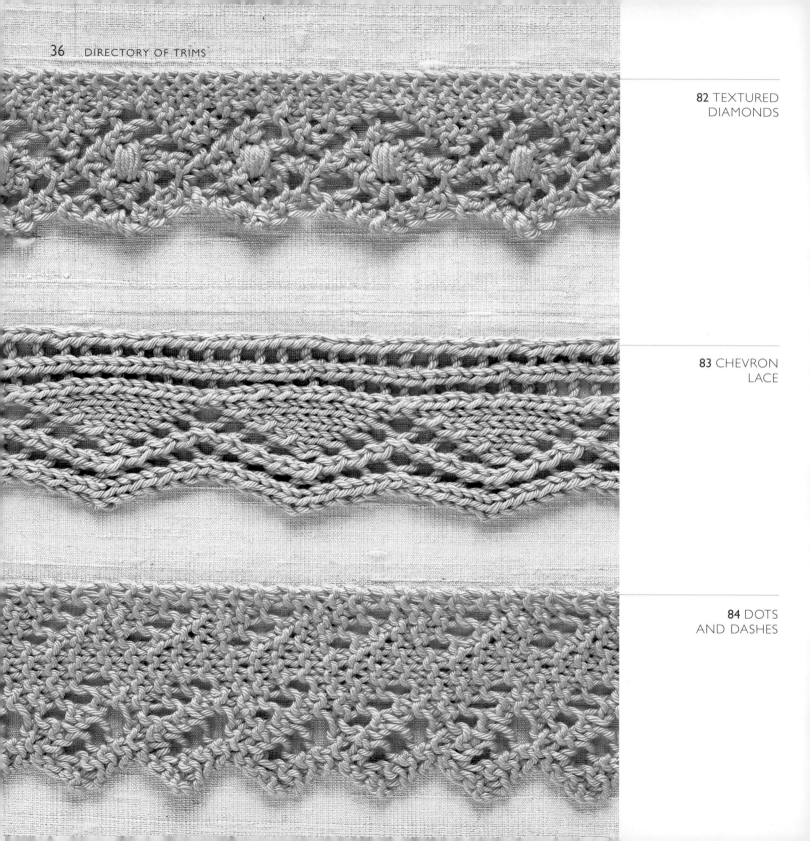

82 TEXTURED
DIAMONDS

83 CHEVRON
LACE

84 DOTS
AND DASHES

85 FISH EYE

86 BLACKBERRY LACE

87 CLASSIC

88 LEAF AND BERRY

89 PENNANTS

90 FERN LEAF

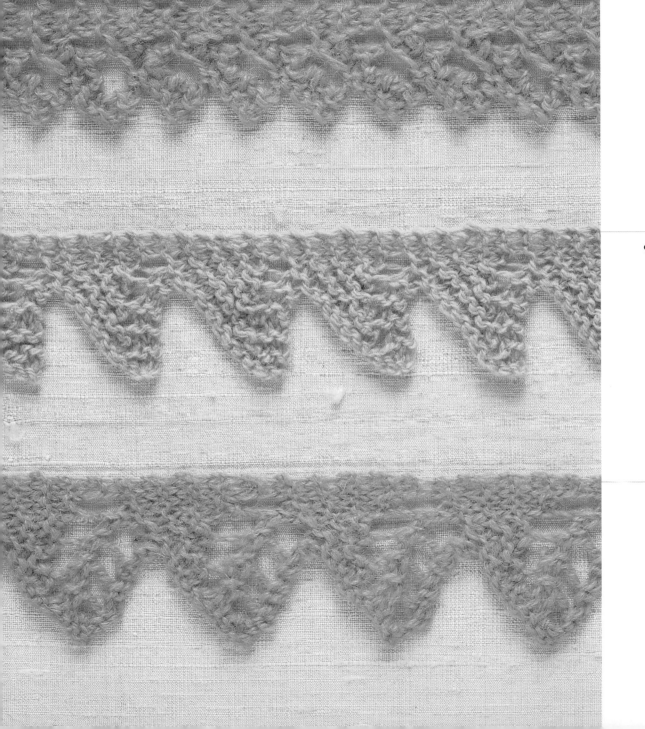

91 PICOT LACE

92 SHARK'S TOOTH

93 WILLOW LEAF

LOOPS AND FRINGES

Knotted tassels and knitted loops can be used for traditional trims or fun embellishment. Some of them may seem slightly tricky to make but most just require a little practice. The style of the result will depend very much on the character of the yarn used—for example, silky loops will be very different from wiry loops. A big, chunky fringe would be very effective as the only decoration on a plain cushion. Sew a fringe with bells on it around a Christmas stocking or add a string of pompoms to the long edge of a scarf.

TO MAKE

For Loops and Fringes instructions, see pages 92–97

94 PICOT LOOPS

95 SEQUIN-TIED FRINGE

96 GARTER STITCH
LOOPS

97 UNRAVELED
FRINGE

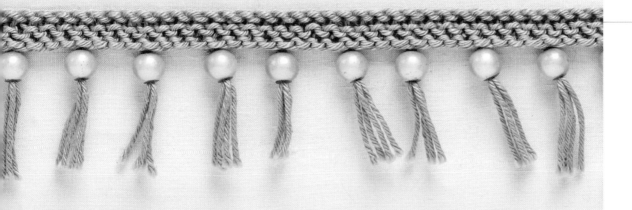

98 BEAD TASSELS

99 BOBBLES

100 KNOTTED
FRINGE

101 EYELETS
AND TASSELS

102 CORD FRINGE

103 TABS

104 LOOP-EDGE
FRINGE

105 SINGLE-LOOP
FRINGE

106 CHAIN PICOT

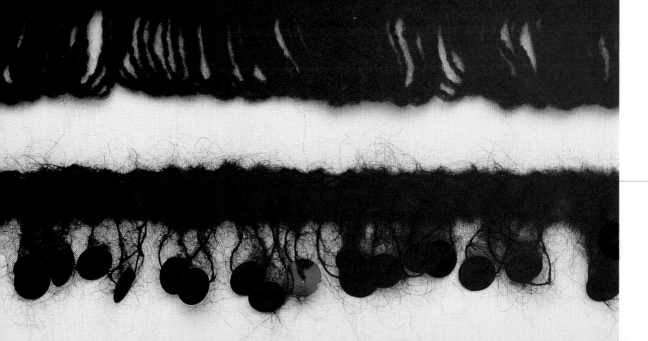

107 DOUBLE
TASSEL HEADS

108 CUT PILE

109 FOLDED
LADDER LOOPS

110 LOOPS AND
SEQUINS

111 LOOPS
AND BELLS

112 POMPOM
FRINGE

113 WILD LOOPS

INSERTIONS

In an age of fine needlework insertions were used as a decorative join between panels of fabric. Today they can still be used in this way, but on a larger scale—say, along the hem of a curtain or blind. An insertion along the top of a lightweight curtain could be gathered directly onto a curtain pole. Threaded with ribbon or cord, an open-eyelet type of insertion will make a casing for a drawstring bag. In a matching or contrasting color, an insertion could be an interesting way to lengthen a jumper.

TO MAKE

For Insertions instructions, see pages 99–104

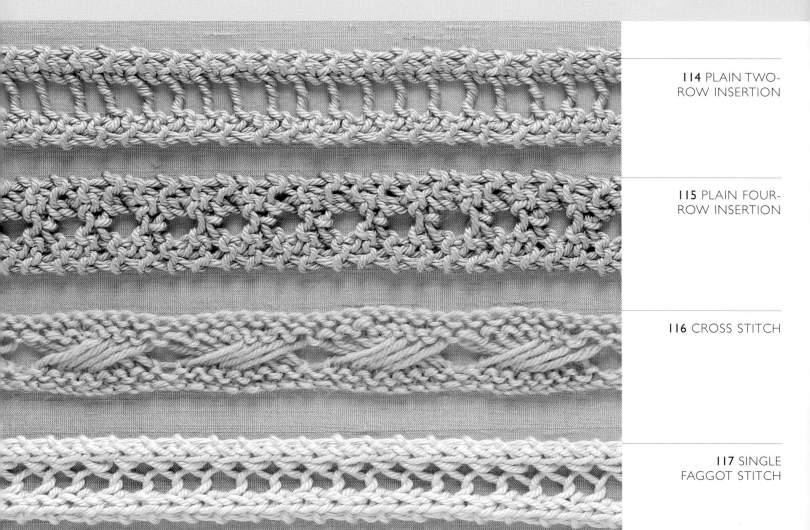

114 PLAIN TWO-ROW INSERTION

115 PLAIN FOUR-ROW INSERTION

116 CROSS STITCH

117 SINGLE FAGGOT STITCH

118 COIN EYELET

119 COCKLESHELL

120 MOCK CABLE

121 DIAGONAL
STRIPE

122 DAISY

123 GARTER-STITCH
DIAMONDS

124 DAISY CHAIN

125 HONEY BEE

126 SKELETON LEAF

127 LACY ZIGZAG

128 TRADITIONAL

129 CHECKERS

ADDITIONS

This miscellany of frivolous things to pin, sew, and appliqué is for knitters who enjoy experimenting on a small scale. The techniques used are mostly quite simple and all the knitting is done with two needles. And it's not difficult to find uses for the additions, or recipients for the presents. You could cluster flowers on a hat, group stars on a T-shirt, hang tiny Christmas stockings on a parcel, tie a knitted bell to the tag of a zipper, and so on.

TO MAKE

For Additions instructions, see pages 105–113

130 BELL

131 ROSE LEAF

132 ROSE

133 ROSEBUD

134 BRAID LEAF

135 LOOP FLOWER

136 FERN LEAF

137 CORNFLOWER

138 BOBBLE

139 BLUE DAISY

140 STAR

141 MARGUERITE

142 HEART

143 BUTTERFLY

144 TUCKED
FLOWER

145 SUNFLOWER

146 BLUEBELLS

147 SNOWDROPS

148 KNITTED TASSEL

149 CORD PULL

150 CHRISTMAS STOCKING

TECHNICAL DATA

This chapter contains all the information you need to make the trims in the directory (pages 14–53). Each set of knitting instructions is accompanied by a list of the materials needed, and a page reference and a trim number to give you its position in the directory. There is also a detailed photograph of the trim so that you can see the stitches.

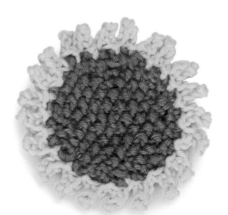

EASY PIECES

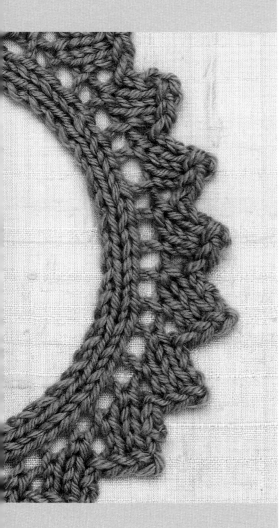

SEE ALSO

Knitting abbreviations, page 9
Refresher course, pages 10–13

 FAGGOT STITCH CORD
Directory view, page 16

Skill level: Easy

 Worsted cotton

 This surprising combination of stitches makes a useful narrow cord.

METHOD

Note: The yarn-over at the beginning of the row is similar to one worked mid-row. The yarn is brought forward from the back, under then over the needle to be in place to make the decrease.

Cast on 2 sts.
1st row Yo, skpo.
Repeat this row throughout.
Bind off.

 GARTER STITCH BRAID
Directory view, page 16

Skill level: Easy

 Sportweight wool

This surprising combination of stitches makes a useful narrow cord. Garter stitch usually has a nubbly edge but these end stitches give a smooth finish.

METHOD

Cast on 6 sts.
1st row With yarn in front, slip one st purlwise, take yarn to the back, k 4, k 1 tbl.
Repeat this row throughout.
Bind off in pattern.

3 CONTRAST PICOT HEM

Directory view, page 16

Skill level: Intermediate

 Sportweight cotton in two shades— light (A) and dark (B)

 A picot hem is particularly decorative if it is outlined with a contrasting shade or color.

METHOD

Note: It may be easier to work the joining row (11th row) with a one-size smaller needle.

With A, cast on an odd number of sts.
1st and 3rd rows K.
2nd row P.
Change to B.
4th row P.
5th row K 1, * yo, k 2 tog; rep from * to end.
This row marks hemline.
Change to A.
6th, 8th, and 10th rows P.
7th and 9th rows K.
11th row Folding hem along 5th row, insert right-hand needle knitwise in first st on left-hand needle and then in loop at base of first st of cast-on edge, k both sts together; work each st on needle with corresponding cast-on st in this way.
Beginning with a p row, continue in stockinette stitch.

4 PICOT POINT

Directory view, page 16

Skill level: Easy

 Worsted wool

 No rows are turned in this trim—it's simply made by casting on and binding off.

METHOD

Note: To cast on 2 sts: k st on left-hand needle but do not slip it off, slip new st from right-hand needle to left-hand needle, inserting needle in space between these 2 sts, k 1 but do not slip it off, transfer new st to left-hand needle.

Make a slip knot on left-hand needle.
* Cast on 2 sts as above, making a total of 3 sts.
Bind off 2 sts.
Slip remaining st from right-hand needle to left-hand needle without twisting it; repeat from * for length required.
Fasten off.

5 STRIPED HEM

Directory view, page 17

Skill level: Intermediate

 Worsted wool in pink (A) and lilac (B)

Two sizes of knitting needles

Stripes are a feature of this hem, but if you prefer, you could knit it in a single color for a different effect.

METHOD

With smaller size needles and A, cast on required number of sts.
1st row K.
2nd row P.
3rd row K.
4th row K to mark hemline.
Change to larger size needles and B.
5th and 7th rows K.
6th and 8th rows P.
Change to smaller size needles and A.
9th row Folding hem along ridge, insert right-hand needle knitwise in first st on left-hand needle and then in loop of first st of cast-on edge, k both sts together; work each st on needle with corresponding cast-on st in this way.
10th row K.
With larger size needles and B, beginning with a k row, continue in stockinette stitch.

6 GARTER STITCH FRINGE
Directory view, page 17

Skill level: Easy

 Worsted cotton

 Simple casting-on and binding-off makes a bold, chunky fringe with lots of uses.

METHOD

*Note: 4th row cast-on: * k first st but do not slip it off, slip new st from right-hand needle onto left-hand needle; inserting needle in space between first and second sts on left-hand needle, repeat from * until 6 new sts have been made.*

Cast on 3 sts.
1st, 2nd, and 3rd rows Slip 1, k 2.
4th row (WS) Cast on 6 sts, bind off 6 sts, k 2. 3 sts.
Repeat 1st–4th rows, ending with a 1st pattern row.
Bind off.

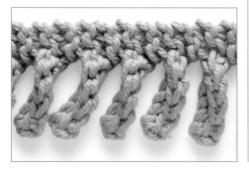

7 FREE TRIANGLES
Directory view, page 17

Skill level: Intermediate

 Sportweight wool

Cable needle

 The garter stitch triangles are made first and then knitted in, so they could be made in different colors to look like little pennants.

METHOD

Triangle (make as many as required)
Put a slip knot on the needle.
1st row (RS) Kfb. 2 sts.
2nd row Kfb, k 1. 3 sts.
3rd row Kfb, k 2. 4 sts.
4th row Kfb, k 3. 5 sts.
5th row Kfb, k 4. 6 sts.
6th row Kfb, k 5. 7 sts.
7th row Kfb, k 6. 8 sts.
8th row Kfb, k 7. 9 sts.
Break yarn and leave sts on a spare needle.
Band Cast on 9 sts.
1st–6th rows Slip 1, k 8.
7th row (RS) Slip 9 sts of one triangle on to cable needle and, right side facing, hold in front of needle with band. Insert right-hand needle in first st on cable needle and k this together with first st on left-hand needle, then slip both sts off together. Work each pair of stitches together in this way.
8th row Slip 1, k 8.
Repeat 1st–8th rows.
Bind off.

8 PICOT BIND-OFF
Directory view, page 17

Skill level: Easy

 Worsted wool in two shades: light (A) and dark (B)

 Casting on two stitches and binding off four stitches results in a decorative picot edge.

METHOD

Note: For a neat rather than a full edge, the last two rows should be worked with a smaller size needle.

With A, cast on an odd number of sts.
Work required depth (in this case, 4 rows garter stitch).
Change to smaller size needle and B.
K 1 row.
Last row (WS) * K next st but do not slip it off, slip new st from right-hand needle on to left-hand needle then make a second new st in this way, bind off 4 sts then slip remaining st back on to left-hand needle; repeat from * to end of row.
Fasten off remaining st.

9 **KNOTTED BRAID**
Directory view, page 17

Skill level: Easy

 Worsted wool *Knots make an attractive texture and are even easier to work than bobbles as there are no turning rows.*

METHOD

Note: To make a knot: (k 1, p 1, k 1, p 1, k 1) in next st, slip 2nd, 3rd, 4th, and 5th of these sts over first st. The multiple increase should not be worked too tightly and the stitches should be slipped carefully one at a time.

Cast on 5 sts.
1st row (RS) Slip 1, k 4.
2nd row As 1st row.
3rd row Slip 1, k 1, make knot, k 2.
4th row As 1st row.
Repeat 1st–4th rows, ending with a second pattern row.
Bind off.

---

 10 **BASIC LACE**
Directory view, page 18

Skill level: Easy

 Worsted wool *The fullness of this lace is due to the yarn-over increases not having corresponding decreases.*

METHOD

Cast on 6 sts.
1st row (RS) Slip 1, k 2, yo, k 3. 7 sts.
2nd row P 6, k 1.
3rd row Slip 1, k 2, yo, k 1, yo, k 3. 9 sts.
4th row Bind off 3 sts purlwise, p 4, k 1. 6 sts.
Repeat 1st–4th rows, ending with a 3rd pattern row.
Bind off.

---

 11 **POINTS**
Directory view, page 18

Skill level: Easy

 Worsted wool *Each point is knitted separately and then joined into a single strip.*

METHOD

Put a slip knot on needle.
1st row (RS) Kfb. 2 sts.
2nd row Kfb, k 1. 3 sts.
3rd row Kfb, k 2. 4 sts.
4th row Kfb, k 3. 5 sts.
Continue to increase one st at the beginning of every row until there are 11 sts.
Break the yarn and leave sts on a spare needle. Make the required number of points without breaking the yarn after the last one.
Next row K 11 sts of last point, with RS facing k each set of 11 sts in turn.
Work 2 rows garter stitch.
Bind off.
Darn in the ends carefully.

12 BABY TEETH
Directory view, page 18

Skill level: Easy

  Sportweight wool The tiny teeth along this edging are just a little larger than a picot.

METHOD

Cast on 5 sts.
1st row (RS) Slip 1, k 4.
2nd row Slip 1, k 4.
3rd row Slip 1, k 1, kfb 3 times. 8 sts.
4th row Bind off 3 sts, k 4. 5 sts.
Repeat 1st–4th rows.
Bind off.

13 TAGS
Directory view, page 18

Skill level: Easy

 Worsted wool Casting on and binding off at regular intervals creates this cut-out effect.

METHOD

Cast on 4 sts.
1st row (WS) Slip 1, k 3.
2nd, 3rd, and 4th rows As first row.
5th row Cast on 3 sts: * k next st but do not slip it off, transfer new st from right-hand needle to left-hand needle; working into new st each time, repeat from * twice; k all 7 sts.
6th, 7th, 8th, 9th, and 10th rows Slip 1, k 6.
11th row Bind off 3 sts, k 3. 4 sts.
12th, 13th, 14th, 15th, 16th, 17th, and 18th rows Slip 1, k 3.
Repeat 5th–18th rows, ending with a 15th pattern row.
Bind off.

14 PICOT SELVEDGE
Directory view, page 19

Skill level: Easy

 Sportweight cotton A picot at the beginning of every row makes bold, decorative edges on a garter stitch band.

METHOD

Cast on 5 sts.
1st row (RS) K.
2nd row Cast on 2 sts: * k in next st but do not slip it off, transfer new st from right-hand to left-hand needle; working into new st, repeat from * once; bind off 2 sts, k 4.
Repeat 2nd row for length required.
Bind off.

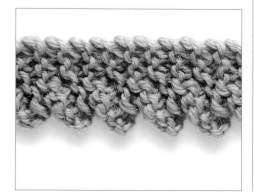

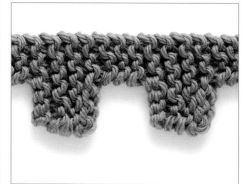

15 CURLY FRINGE
Directory view, page 19

Skill level: Intermediate

 Worsted wool

 This is a variation on the Garter Stitch Fringe (see page 58), with increases causing the fringe to twist.

METHOD

Cast on 3 sts.
1st, 2nd, and 3rd rows K.
4th row (WS) Cast on 10 sts: * k in next st but do not slip it off, transfer new st from right-hand to left-hand needle; working into new st, repeat from * 9 times; do not turn, kfb in each of these 10 sts binding off one st as each st is made, k 2. 3 sts.
Repeat 1st–4th rows, ending with a 2nd row.
Bind off.

16 OPEN PICOT
Directory view, page 19

Skill level: Easy

 Worsted cotton

 Here, a string of picot point is made and then worked into along its length with garter stitch.

METHOD

Put a slip knot on needle.
** Cast on 2 sts: * k in st but do not slip it off, transfer new st from right-hand to left-hand needle; working into new st, repeat from * once. 3 sts.
Bind off 2 sts. 1 st.
Slip this st on to left-hand needle.
Repeat from ** for required length.
Without turning, work along straight edge of picot: * yo, k in loop of picot; repeat from * to end.
K 2 rows.
Bind off.

17 SAW TOOTH
Directory view, page 19

Skill level: Easy

 Worsted wool

 Instead of the more usual series of increases followed by binding off, this indented edging combines decreases with casting on.

METHOD

*Note: On 10th row cast on 4 sts: * k next st but do not slip it off, transfer new st from right-hand to left-hand needle; repeat from * 3 times, working into new st each time.*

Cast on 8 sts.
1st row (RS) Slip 1, k 7.
2nd row K 2 tog, k 6. 7 sts.
3rd row Slip 1, k 6.
4th row K 2 tog, k 5. 6 sts.
5th row Slip 1, k 5.
6th row K 2 tog, k 4. 5 sts.
7th row Slip 1, k 4.
8th row K 2 tog, k 3. 4 sts.
9th row Slip 1, k 3.
10th row Cast on 4 sts as above, k all 8 sts.
Repeat 1st–10th rows, ending with a
9th pattern row.
Bind off.

18 BUTTON BAND

Directory view, page 19

Skill level: Easy

 Worsted wool

 Buttons

 This is a simple seed stitch band with buttons stitched on. The method for making buttonholes is explained, but these are optional.

METHOD

With yarn used double, cast on an odd number of sts. Continue with single yarn.
1st row K 1, * p 1, k 1; repeat from * to end.
Repeat this row 8 times.
Bind off in pattern.
Sew on buttons.

Buttonhole (optional)

The most usual way to make a buttonhole is to bind off a number of sts on one row and replace them with cast-on sts on the next. This method of casting on is simple and sturdy: work to the bound-off sts, turn, cast on replacement stitches: * k in next st but do not slip it off, transfer new st from right-hand to left-hand needle; working into space between sts, repeat from * but before transferring the last st to the left-hand needle bring the yarn to the front, turn, continue along the row.

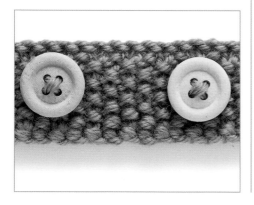

19 LOOP SELVEDGE

Directory view, page 20

Skill level: Easy

 Fine mohair

 A yarn-over loop at the beginning of each row is the only decoration on this garter stitch band.

METHOD

Cast on 7 sts.
1st row Bring yarn forward underneath the right-hand needle and take it over the needle loosely, then k 2 tog, k 5.
Repeat this row.
Bind off.
Pin out each loop before pressing.

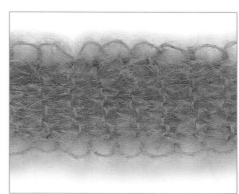

20 PIPING

Directory view, page 20

Skill level: Intermediate

 Worsted cotton

A single long tuck can be inserted in a seam in exactly the same way as conventional piping.

METHOD

Cast on required number of sts.
1st row (RS) K.
2nd row P.
3rd row K.
4th row K.
5th row P.
6th row K.
7th row P.
8th row K.
9th row * Insert right-hand needle in first st and then in back loop of first st on 6th row below (edge of reverse stockinette stitch), k both sts together; repeat from * to join each st on needle with corresponding st of 6th row below.
10th row P.
11th row K.
Bind off.

21 SEED STITCH BRAID
Directory view, page 20

Skill level: Easy

 Worsted cotton   *This narrow band of seed stitch has a smooth slip-stitch edge.*

METHOD

Cast on 5 sts.
1st row With yarn in front slip one st purlwise, take yarn to back, k 1, p 1, k 1, k 1 tbl.
Repeat this row throughout.
Bind off in pattern.

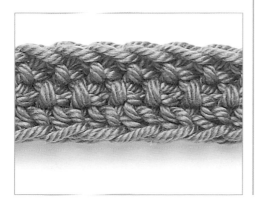

---

 22 BIAS BINDING
Directory view, page 20

Skill level: Easy

 Worsted cotton   *The diagonal slant of this stockinette binding is made by decreasing at one edge and increasing at the other.*

METHOD

Cast on 10 sts.
1st row (WS) P.
2nd row K 1, k 2 tog, k 6, make a st by picking up strand in front of next st and k in back of it, k 1.
Repeat 1st and 2nd rows, ending with a 1st pattern row.
Bind off purlwise.

---

23 KNOTTED EDGE
Directory view, page 20

Skill level: Intermediate

Worsted cotton *This is one of the cast-ons used for traditional Channel Island Guernseys. The explanation looks complicated but it's very similar to casting on by the thumb method (see page 10)*

METHOD

Double the end of the yarn so that it's approximately three times the length of the cast-on required.
Starting a short distance from where double and single yarn meet, wind doubled yarn counterclockwise around left thumb twice. Using doubled yarn, k yarn on thumb to make first st. Make second st the same. Now drop end of yarn and use single yarn in right hand as follows: * yarn forward and over needle to make a st, wind doubled yarn counterclockwise around left thumb twice and k into these strands to make a st; repeat from * for required length. This will form the right side of an even number of sts, the first two being double.
For a traditional edging continue in garter stitch.

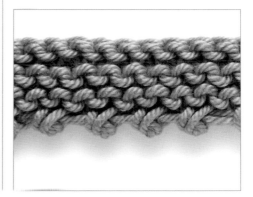

24 BEADED CAST-ON

Directory view, page 21

Skill level: Intermediate

 Sportweight wool

 Small beads, sewing needle, and strong thread

 Beads can be worked into the cast-on edge of almost any stitch—here they have been used with simple twisted rib.

METHOD

Thread beads onto knitting yarn
(see page 13), one for each alternate stitch.
To cast on: leaving a sufficiently long end put
a slip knot on the needle above the threaded
beads, * slide a bead along the yarn and up
against the needle before making a loop on
the thumb to cast on one st by the thumb
method (see page 10), then cast on one st
without a bead; repeat from * to end, making
an odd number of sts.
1st row (WS) K 1, * p 1 tbl, k 1; repeat from
* to end.
2nd row P 1, * k 1 tbl, p 1; repeat from
* to end.
Repeat 1st and 2nd rows once, then
1st row again.
Bind off in rib.

25 BEADED LOOP EDGING

Directory view, page 21

Skill level: Intermediate

 Sportweight cotton

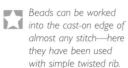 *Assorted beads, sewing needle, and strong thread*

 Suspend a bead on a loop at the beginning of alternate right-side rows to decorate an otherwise plain garter stitch band.

METHOD

Thread beads onto knitting yarn
(see page 13).
Cast on 5 sts.
1st row (RS) Slip 1, k 4.
2nd row As 1st row.
3rd row Push a bead up to the left-hand
needle and with left thumb hold it against
needle, with yarn to front, insert right-hand
needle in back of first 2 sts, take yarn over
needle and k 2 tog tbl, k 3.
4th row Slip 1, k 3, k loop as if it were a st.
Repeat 1st–4th rows.
Bind off.

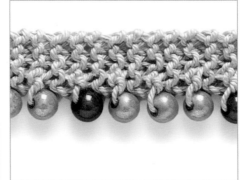

26 NARROW BEADED BRAID

Directory view, page 21

Skill level: Intermediate

 Sportweight cotton

 *Medium-size beads, sewing needle, and strong thread*

Here a single bead is held in front of a slip stitch on a garter stitch background.

METHOD

Thread beads onto knitting yarn
(see page 13).
Cast on 5 sts.
1st row (RS) Slip 1, k 4.
2nd row As 1st row.
3rd row Slip 1, k 1, bring yarn to front, slide
bead up to needle, slip next st purlwise, take
yarn to back, tension yarn then k 2.
4th row Slip 1, k 4.
Repeat 1st–4th rows, ending with a
1st pattern row.
Bind off.

27 WIDE BEADED BRAID
Directory view, page 21

Skill level: Intermediate

 Sportweight cotton

 Small beads, sewing needle, and strong thread

 Slipping a stitch and taking a bead across in front is all it takes to create this richly textured surface.

METHOD

Note: bead 1: bring yarn to front, slide bead up to needle, slip next st purlwise, take yarn to back, tension yarn before working next st.

Thread beads onto knitting yarn
(see page 13).
Cast on 9 sts.
1st row (RS) Slip 1, k 1, [bead 1, k 1]
3 times, k 1.
2nd row Slip 1, p 7, k 1.
3rd row Slip 1, [bead 1, k 1] 4 times.
4th row As 2nd row.
Repeat 1st–4th rows.
Bind off.

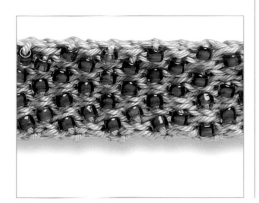

28 BIRD'S EYE
Directory view, page 21

Skill level: Easy

 Worsted wool

This is a simple, bold combination of scallops and eyelets, all in garter stitch.

METHOD

Cast on 4 sts.
1st row (RS) K 2, yo 3 times, k 2. 7 sts.
2nd row K 3, p 1, k 3.
3rd, 4th, and 5th rows K.
6th row Slipping first st, bind off 3 sts,
k 3. 4 sts.
Repeat 1st–6th rows.
Bind off.

BRAIDS

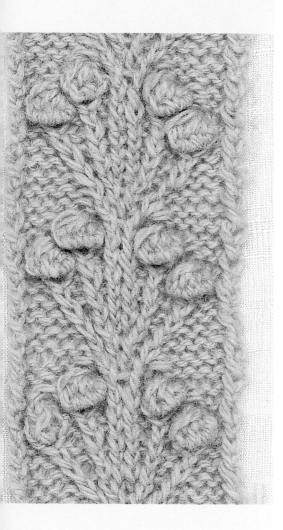

 ## 29 ZIGZAG RIB
Directory view, page 22

Skill level: Easy

 Worsted cotton

 Twisting two stitches on both right-side and wrong-side rows makes a strong zigzag ridge.

METHOD

Cast on 4 sts.
1st row (RS) K 1, take right-hand needle to the back and k second st through the back of the loop, then k first st in the usual way, slip both sts off together, k 1.
2nd row K 1, with yarn to the front miss first st and p second st, then p first st, slip both sts off together, k 1.
Repeat 1st and 2nd rows.
Bind off.

30 SMALL CHAIN
Directory view, page 22

Skill level: Easy

 Worsted cotton
Cable needle

 Cabling on every right-side row transforms four stitches into a tight chain.

METHOD

Cast on 6 sts.
1st row (WS) Slip 1, p 4, k 1.
2nd row Slip 1, slip next st onto cable needle and hold at back, k 1 then k 1 from cable needle, slip next st onto cable needle and hold at front, k 1 then k 1 from cable needle, k 1.
3rd row As 1st row.
4th row Slip 1, slip next st onto cable needle and hold at front, k 1 then k 1 from cable needle, slip next st onto cable needle and hold at back, k 1 then k 1 from cable needle, k 1.
Repeat 1st–4th rows.
Bind off.

SEE ALSO

Knitting abbreviations, page 9
Refresher course, pages 10–13

31 ### LAMBS' TAILS
Directory view, page 22

Skill level: Easy

 Worsted cotton

 Little lamb's tail loops sit in a tidy row or tumble about, according to the yarn used.

METHOD

Cast on 5 sts.
1st row (WS) Slip 1, k 4.
2nd row Slip 1, k 1, [k in next st but do not slip it off, transfer st just made from right-hand needle to left-hand needle] 3 times to make 3 new sts, bind off 3 sts, k 2. 5 sts.
Repeat 1st and 2nd rows.
Bind off.

---

32 ### ROPE
Directory view, page 22

Skill level: Intermediate

 Worsted wool
Cable needle

 A loop edging is added to a classic rope cable.

METHOD

Note: c4b—slip next 2 sts onto cable needle and hold at back, k2 then k2 from cable needle; m1—make a st by picking up strand in front of next st and k in back of it; yo—bring yarn forward underneath the right-hand needle and take it over the needle loosely.

Cast on 7 sts.
Increase row K 3, m 1, k 4. 8 sts.
Now pattern:
1st row (WS) Yo, k 2 tog, p 4, k 2.
2nd row Yo, k 2 tog, k 6.
3rd row As 1st row.
4th row Yo, k 2 tog, c4b, k 2.
Repeat 1st–4th rows, ending with a 1st pattern row.
Bind off, working k 4, k 2 tog, k 2 across the row.

---

33 ### BOBBLE AND RIB
Directory view, page 23

Skill level: Intermediate

 Sportweight cotton

These bobbles are actually small tucks so they have a firm, square shape.

METHOD

Note: b 1—make bobble: [k 3, turn, p 3, turn] 3 times, yarn to back, insert left-hand needle in back loop of first st of first row of bobble, k this tog with first st on needle, k 1, insert left-hand needle in last st of first row of bobble, k this together with next st on needle.

Cast on 7 sts.
1st row (RS) K 1, [k 1 tbl, p 1] twice, k 1 tbl, k 1.
2nd row K 1, [p 1 tbl, k 1] 3 times.
3rd row K 1, k 1 tbl, b 1, k 1 tbl, k 1.
4th row As 2nd row.
Repeat 1st–4th rows, ending with a 1st pattern row.
Bind off in rib.

34 WIDE BRAID
Directory view, page 23

Skill level: Easy

 Worsted cotton
Cable needle

 Braided cables are a wonderful deception—they look complex but are really very easy.

METHOD

Note: c4b—slip next 2 sts onto cable needle and hold at back, k2 then k2 from cable needle; c4f—slip next 2 sts onto cable needle and hold at front, k2 then k2 from cable needle.

Cast on 10 sts.
1st row (WS) Slip 1, p 8, k 1.
2nd row Slip 1, c4b twice, k 1.
3rd row As 1st row.
4th row Slip 1, k 2, c4f, k 3.
Repeat 1st–4th rows, ending with a 3rd pattern row.
Bind off, working k 3, k 2 tog, k 2, k 2 tog, k 1 across row.

35 CARTRIDGE BELT
Directory view, page 23

Skill level: Intermediate

 Sportweight wool

 Four-row bands of reverse stocking stitch, each gathered up into a tuck, make these rounded ridges.

METHOD

Cast on 6 sts.
1st row (WS) P.
2nd row K.
3rd row P.
4th row P.
5th row K.
6th row P.
7th row K.
8th row * Insert needle in first st and then in back loop of first st on 5th row below, k both sts tog; repeat from * to join each st on needle with corresponding st of ridge below.
Repeat 1st–8th rows, ending with a 3rd pattern row.
Bind off.

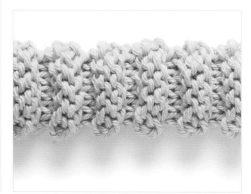

36 CLUSTERED BEADS
Directory view, page 23

Skill level: Easy

 Sportweight cotton

 Beads, sewing needle, and strong thread

 Using sewing needle and strong thread, thread beads onto knitting yarn (see page 13).

METHOD

Note: bead 1—bring yarn to front, slide bead up to needle, slip next st purlwise, take yarn to back, tension yarn before working next st.

Cast on 7 sts.
1st and 3rd rows (RS) Slip 1, k 6.
2nd and 4th rows Slip 1, p 5, k 1.
5th row Slip 1, k 2, bead 1, k 3.
6th row As 2nd row.
7th row Slip 1, k 1, bead 1, k 1, bead 1, k 2.
8th row As 2nd row.
9th row As 5th row.
10th row As 2nd row.
Repeat 1st–10th rows, ending with a 2nd pattern row.
Bind off.

37 STRIPED BIAS BRAID

Directory view, page 23

Skill level: Easy

 Worsted wool in dark (A) and light (B)

 Because of the diagonal slant of each end, this braid is suited to being joined in a continuous band.

METHOD

Note: m 1—make a st by picking up strand in front of next st and k in back of it.

With A, cast on 5 sts.
1st row (RS) With A, k 2 tog, k 2, m 1, k 1.
2nd row P.
3rd row With B, k 2 tog, k 2, m 1, k 1.
4th row P.
Repeat 1st–4th rows, without breaking yarn between stripes. Carry yarn not in use along the side edge, taking the dark shade in front of the light shade each time.
Bind off.

38 SEQUIN BRAID

Directory view, page 23

Skill level: Intermediate

 Fine mohair

Sequins

 A straight line of sequins is knitted into a garter stitch band of fine mohair.

METHOD

Note: Each sequin is knitted on a right-side row and when the stitch has been completed should lie flat against the needle on that row. Thread the sequins directly onto the yarn if possible (see page 13).

Cast on 5 sts.
1st row (RS) Slip 1, k 4.
2nd row As 1st row.
3rd row Slip 1, k 1, push a sequin along yarn until it is flat against needle on WS, k next st pushing sequin through the loop of st being dropped from left-hand needle, tension yarn to bring sequin close to needle, then k next 2 sts.
4th row Slip 1, k 4.
Repeat 3rd and 4th rows.
Bind off.

39 CHAIN

Directory view, page 24

Skill level: Easy

Worsted wool
Cable needle

Familiar four-stitch cables texture this chunky braid.

METHOD

Note: c4b—slip next 2 sts onto cable needle and hold at back, k2 then k2 from cable needle; c4f—slip next 2 sts onto cable needle and hold at front, k2 then k2 from cable needle.

Cast on 12 sts.
1st row (RS) Slip 1, p 1, k 8, p 1, k 1.
2nd, 4th, and 6th rows Slip 1, k 1, p 8, k 2.
3rd row Slip 1, p 1, c4b, c4f, p 1, k 1.
5th row As 1st row.
7th row Slip 1, p 1, c4f, c4b, p 1, k 1.
8th row As 2nd row.
Repeat 1st–8th rows
Bind off.

BLACKBERRY
Directory view, page 24

Skill level: Easy

 Worsted wool

 Usually an all-over pattern, a narrow band of blackberry stitch makes an attractive braid.

METHOD

Cast on 5 sts.
1st row (RS) P.
2nd row (K 1, p 1, k 1) in first st, p 3 tog, (k 1, p 1, k 1) in last st. 7 sts.
3rd row P.
4th row P 3 tog, (k 1, p 1, k 1) in next st, p 3 tog. 5 sts.
Repeat 1st–4th rows.
Bind off.

KNOP FLOWER
Directory view, page 24

Skill level: Intermediate

 Sportweight cotton

 Both the raised pattern and the background of this braid are in garter stitch.

METHOD

Note: b 1—make bobble: (k 1, p 1, k 1, p 1, k 1) in next st, [turn, k 5] twice, slip 2nd, 3rd, 4th, and 5th sts on right-hand needle one at a time over first st.

Cast on 9 sts.
1st, 2nd, 3rd, 4th, 5th, and 6th rows Slip 1, k 8.
7th row (RS) Slip 1, k 3, b 1, k 4.
8th, 9th, and 10th rows Slip 1, k 8.
11th row Slip 1, k 1, b 1, k 3, b 1, k 2.
12th, 13th, and 14th rows Slip 1, k 8.
15th row As 7th row.
16th row Slip 1, k 8.
Repeat 1st–16th rows, ending with a 6th pattern row.
Bind off.

KNOTTED CABLE
Directory view, page 24

Skill level: Intermediate

 Sportweight wool Cable needle

An unusual cable cross appears to knot each link of this chain.

METHOD

Cast on 12 sts.
1st and 3rd rows (RS) Slip 1, k 1, p 1, k 2, p 2, k 2, p 1, k 2.
2nd and 4th rows Slip 1, [k 2, p 2] twice, k 3.
5th row Slip 1, k 1, p 1, slip next 4 sts onto cable needle and hold at front, k 2 then slip 2 sts from cable needle back onto left-hand needle, take cable needle to back of work, p 2 from left-hand needle, k 2 from cable needle, p 1, k 2.
6th row As 2nd row.
7th row As 1st row.
8th row As 2nd row.
Repeat 1st–8th rows.
Bind off in pattern.

43 POSY

Directory view, page 24

Skill level: Complex

 2-ply Jumper Weight Shetland wool

Cable needle

These tight little bundles of flowers require cabling on right-side and wrong-side rows.

METHOD

Note: b 1—make bobble: (k 1, p 1, k 1, p 1, k 1) in next st, turn, p 5, turn, slip 2nd, 3rd, 4th, and 5th over first st, then k this st tbl; c2b—slip 1 st onto cable needle and hold at back, k 1 tbl then k 1 tbl from cable needle; c2f—slip 1 st onto cable needle and hold at front, k 1 tbl then k 1 tbl from cable needle; c2bp—slip 1 st onto cable needle and hold at back, on RS rows k 1 tbl then p 1 from cable needle, on WS rows k 1 then p 1 tbl from cable needle; c2fp—slip 1 st onto cable needle and hold at front, on RS rows p 1 then k 1 tbl from cable needle, on WS rows p 1 tbl then k 1 from cable needle.

Cast on 18 sts.

1st row (WS) P 1 tbl, k 7, p 2 tbl, k 7, p 1 tbl.

2nd row K 1 tbl, p 6, c2b, c2f, p 6, k 1 tbl.

3rd row P 1 tbl, k 5, c2fp, p 2 tbl, c2bp, k 5, p 1 tbl.

4th row K 1 tbl, p 4, c2bp, c2b, c2f, c2fp, p 4, k 1 tbl.

5th row P 1 tbl, k 3, c2fp, k 1, p 4 tbl, k 1, c2bp, k 3, p 1 tbl.

6th row K 1 tbl, p 2, c2bp, p 1, c2bp, k 2 tbl, c2fp, p 1, c2fp, p 2, k 1 tbl.

7th row P 1 tbl, [k 2, p 1 tbl] twice, k 1, p 2 tbl, k 1, [p 1 tbl, k 2] twice, p 1 tbl.

8th row K 1 tbl, p 2, b 1, p 1, c2bp, p 1, k 2 tbl, p 1, c2fp, p 1, b 1, p 2, k 1 tbl.

9th row P 1 tbl, k 4, p 1 tbl, k 2, p 2 tbl, k 2, p 1 tbl, k 4, p 1 tbl.

10th row K 1 tbl, p 4, b 1, p 2, k 2 tbl, p 2, b 1, p 4, k 1 tbl.

Repeat 1st–10th rows.
Bind off.

44 BUD AND STEM

Directory view, page 25

Skill level: Intermediate

 Worsted wool

 A multiple increase followed by gradual decreases shapes the buds on this curvy braid.

METHOD

Note: sk2po—slip one st knitwise, k 2 tog, pass slipped st over.

Cast on 7 sts.

1st row (RS) K 1 tbl, [p 2, k 1 tbl] twice.

2nd row P 1, [k 2, p 1 tbl] twice.

3rd row K 1 tbl, p 2, (k 1, p 1, k 1, p 1, k 1) in next st, p 2, k 1 tbl. 11 sts.

4th row P 1, k 2, p 5, k 2, p 1 tbl.

5th row K 1 tbl, p 2, k 5, p 2, k 1 tbl.

6th row As 4th row.

7th row K 1 tbl, p 2, skpo, k 1, k 2 tog, p 2, k 1 tbl. 9 sts.

8th row P 1, k 2, p 3, k 2, p 1 tbl.

9th row K 1 tbl, p 2, sk2po, p 2, k 1 tbl. 7 sts.

10th row As 2nd row.

Repeat 1st–10th rows, ending with a 1st pattern row.
Bind off in pattern.

45 BAY LEAF

Directory view, page 25

Skill level: Intermediate

 Sportweight wool

 A highly embossed leaf is made by building up increases and then working the decreases separately.

METHOD

Note: m1p—make a st by picking up a strand in front of next st and p in back of it; sk2po—slip 1 st, k 2 tog, pass slipped st over.

Cast on 13 sts.
1st row (RS) Slip 1, k 2, p 2, [k 1, yo] twice, k 1, p 2, k 3. 15 sts.
2nd row Slip 1, k 4, p 5, k 5.
3rd row Slip 1, k 2, p 2, k 2, yo, k 1, yo, k 2, p 2, k 3. 17 sts.
4th row Slip 1, k 4, p 7, k 5.
5th row Slip 1, k 2, p 2, k 3, yo, k 1, yo, k 3, p 2, k 3. 19 sts.
6th row Slip 1, k 4, p 9, k 5.
7th row Slip 1, k 2, p 2, k 4, yo, k 1, yo, k 4, p 2, k 3. 21 sts.
8th row Slip 1, k 4, p 11, k 5.
9th row Slip 1, k 2, p 2, k 11, p 2, k 3.
10th row As 8th row.

11th row Slip 1, k 2, p 2, skpo, k 7, k 2 tog, p 2, k3. 19 sts.
12th row As 6th row.
13th row Slip 1, k 2, p 2, skpo, k 5, k 2 tog, p 2, k 3. 17 sts.
14th row As 4th row.
15th row Slip 1, k 2, p 2, skpo, k 3, k 2 tog, p 2, k 3. 15 sts.
16th row As 2nd row.
17th row Slip 1, k 2, p 2, skpo, k 1, k 2 tog, p 2, k 3. 13 sts.
18th row Slip 1, k 4, p 3, k 5.
19th row Slip 1, k 2, p 2, m1p, sk2po, m1p, p 2, k 3.
20th row Slip 1, k 5, p 1, k 6.
Repeat 1st–20th rows.
Bind off.

46 EMBOSSED BRAID

Directory view, page 25

Skill level: Intermediate

 Worsted wool
Cable needle

 It's so three dimensional this braid makes other cables look flat. Turning rows enhance each cable cross.

METHOD

Cast on 11 sts.
Increase row Slip 1, k 1, p 4, [p in front and back of next st] twice, p 1, k 2. 13 sts.
Now pattern:
1st row (RS) Slip 1, p 1, k 6, [turn, p 3, turn, k 3] twice, slip these sts onto cable needle and leave at front, take yarn between needles to back, slip 3 sts from right-hand needle to left-hand needle, k 6, p 1, k 1.
2nd row Slip 1, k 1, p 6, p 3 from cable needle, k 2.
3rd row Slip 1, p 1, k 6, [turn, p 3, turn, k 3] twice, slip these 3 sts onto cable needle and leave at front, take yarn between needles to back, slip 3 sts from left-hand needle to right-hand needle, p 1, k 1.

4th row Slip 1, k 1, p 3 from cable needle, p 6, k 2.
Repeat 1st–4th rows.
Bind off, working slip 1, p 1, k 2, skpo, k 1, k 2 tog, k 2, p 1, k 1 across row.

47 TWILL
Directory view, page 25

Skill level: Intermediate

 Sportweight wool

 This twist-stitch knitting imitates a twill fabric ribbon.

METHOD

Note: t2r—twist 2 sts to the right: k 2 tog leaving sts on needle, insert right-hand needle between sts just worked and k first st again, slip both sts off together.

Cast on 12 sts.
1st row (WS) Slip 1, k 1, p 8, k 2.
2nd row Slip 1, p 1, t2r 4 times, p 1, k 1.
3rd row Slip 1, k 1, p 8, k 2.
4th row Slip 1, p 1, k 1, t2r 3 times, k 1, p 1, k 1.
Repeat 1st–4th rows.
Bind off.

48 RICKRACK
Directory view, page 25

Skill level: Intermediate

 Sportweight wool

 Garter stitch chevrons make a fun zigzag trim. To estimate length, first knit a small sample.

METHOD

Note: m1—make a st by picking up strand in front of next st and k in back of it; s2kpo—slip 2 sts as if to k 2 tog, k 1, pass slipped sts over.

Cast on a multiple of 10 sts plus 1.
1st row (RS) K 4, * s2kpo, k 7; repeat from *, ending s2kpo, k 4. Multiple of 8 sts plus 1.
2nd, 4th, and 6th rows K.
3rd row K 1, * m1, k 2, s2kpo, k 2, m1, k 1; repeat from * to end.
5th row As 3rd row.
7th row Bind off, working k 1, * m1, k 7, m1, k 1; repeat from * across row.

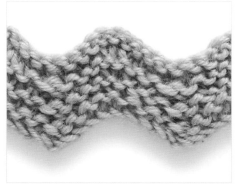

FRILLS AND FLOUNCES

SEE ALSO

Knitting abbreviations, page 9
Refresher course, pages 10–13

49 WAVES

Directory view, page 26

Skill level: Intermediate

 Sportweight wool

 These waves are similar to Feather and fan (page 81) but without the lacy element.

METHOD

Cast on a multiple of 12 sts.
1st row (RS) K.
2nd row P.
3rd row * K 2 tog twice, [m 1, k 1] 4 times, skpo twice; repeat from * to end.
4th row P.
5th row * K 2 tog twice, k 4, skpo twice; repeat from * to end.
6th row K.
7th row K.
Bind off.

50 SCALLOPS

Directory view, page 26

Skill level: Intermediate

 Worsted wool

 Perhaps it's not quite as simple as it looks, but this edging uses garter stitch to great effect.

METHOD

Note: Increases are made on wrong-side rows and decreases are made on right-side rows.

Cast on 5 sts.
1st row (RS) K.
2nd row Kfb twice, k 3. 7 sts.
3rd row K.
4th row Kfb twice, k 5. 9 sts.
5th, 6th, 7th, and 8th rows K.
9th row K 5, k 2 tog twice. 7 sts.
10th row K.
11th row K 3, k 2 tog twice. 5 sts.
12th row K.
Repeat 1st–12th rows.
Bind off.

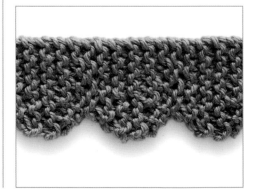

51 BOX PLEATS
Directory view, page 26

Skill level: Complex

 Sportweight wool
Two additional double-pointed needles

 Joining the pleats at the top by knitting three sets of stitches together is a little tricky but the resulting crisp pleats are very effective.

METHOD

Note: Slipping a st purlwise with the yarn in front (wyf) makes an inside fold and slipping a st purlwise with the yarn at the back (wyb) makes an outside fold.

Cast on a multiple of 24 sts.
1st row (RS) K 4, * sl 1 wyf, k 3, sl 1 wyb, k 6, sl 1 wyb, k 3, sl 1 wyf, k 8; repeat from *, ending k 4.
2nd row P.
Repeat 1st and 2nd rows 5 times.
13th row Join pleats: * [slip next 4 sts onto a double-pointed needle] twice, fold along slip sts so that left hand needle and double-pointed needles are parallel, then, taking one st from each needle, [k 3 tog] 4 times; repeat from *, folding to make box pleats.
14th and 15th rows K.
Bind off.

52 LACY FLUTES
Directory view, page 27

Skill level: Intermediate

 Sportweight wool

 Rows of eyelets emphasize the lines of this full, fluted edging.

METHOD

Note: To prevent a hole when turning to work a short row, wrap the yarn around the next stitch like this: turn, leaving the yarn at the front, slip the first st from the right-hand needle to the left-hand needle, take the yarn to the back, slip the st back on to the right-hand needle, then continue.

Cast on 14 sts.
1st row (RS) K 2, p 9, k 3.
2nd row Slip 1, k 2, [k 2 tog, yo] 4 times, k 1, yo, k 2 tog.
3rd row K 2, p 9, k 3.
4th row Slip 1, k 2, p 9, yo, k 2 tog.
5th row K 11, turn, p 9, yo, k 2 tog, turn.
6th row K 2, p 9, turn, p 9, yo, k 2 tog, turn.
Repeat 1st–6th rows, ending with a 3rd pattern row.
Bind off.

53 CROCHET-TRIMMED FRILL
Directory view, page 27

Skill level: Complex

 Sportweight wool
Crochet hook

 There's no bind-off row on this edging—the final loops are made with crochet.

METHOD

Note: sk2po—slip one st knitwise, k 2 tog, pass slipped st over.

Cast on a multiple of 3 sts plus 1.
1st, 2nd, and 3rd rows K.
4th row P.
5th row (RS) K 2 tog, * yo twice, sk2po; repeat from * to last 2 sts, yo twice, skpo.
6th row * P 2, k 1; repeat from * to last st, p 1.
Repeat 5th and 6th rows 3 times.
13th row Substituting crochet hook for right-hand needle, insert hook in back of first 2 sts, yarn round hook, draw yarn through 2 sts, make 9 chain, * insert hook in back of next 3 sts, yarn round hook, draw yarn through all 4 loops, make 9 chain; repeat from *, ending insert hook in back of last 2 sts, yarn round hook, draw yarn through all 3 loops.
Fasten off.

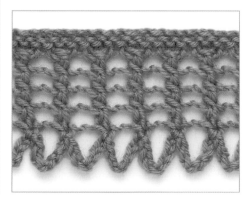

54 UMBRELLA FLOUNCE
Directory view, page 27

Skill level: Intermediate

Worsted wool

 An adaptation of a well-known repeat pattern makes a crisp, curvy edging.

METHOD

Cast on a multiple of 18 sts plus 1.
1st row (RS) P.
2nd row P 2, * [k 3, p 1] 3 times, k 3, p 3; rep from *, ending p 2.
3rd row K 1, * yo, k 1, p 2 tog, p 1, [k 1, p 3] twice, k 1, p 1, p 2 tog, k 1, yo, k1; rep from * to end.
4th row P 3, * k 2, [p 1, k 3] twice, p 1, k 2, p 5; rep from *, ending p 3.
5th row K 2, * yo, k 1, p 2, [k 1, p 1, p 2 tog] twice, k 1, p 2, k 1, yo, k 3; rep from *, ending k 2.
6th row P 4, *[k 2, p 1] 3 times, k 2, p7; rep from *, ending p 4.
7th row K 3, * yo, k 1, p 2 tog, [k 1, p 2] twice, k 1, p 2 tog, k 1, yo, k 5; rep from *, ending k 3.

8th row P 5, * k 1, [p 1, k 2] twice, p 1, k 1, p 9; rep from *, ending p 5.
9th row K 4, * yo, k 1, p 1, [k 1, p 2 tog] twice, k 1, p 1, k 1, yo, k 7; rep from *, ending k 4.
10th row P 6, * k 1, [p 1, k 1] 3 times, p 11; rep from *, ending p 6.
11th row K 5, * skpo twice, k 1, k 2 tog twice, k 9; rep from *, ending k 5. Multiple of 14 sts plus 1.
K 2 rows.
Bind off.

---

 55 SEA SPRAY
Directory view, page 27

Skill level: Complex

Sportweight wool

 The open eyelets along the edge of this trim add fullness as well as decoration.

METHOD

Cast on 8 sts.
1st row (RS) Slip 1, k 5, yo twice, k 2 tog. 9 sts.
2nd, 4th, 6th, 8th, 10th, 12th, and 14th rows P 2, k to end.
3rd row Slip 1, k to end.
5th row Slip 1, k 6, yo twice, k 2 tog. 10 sts.
7th row As 3rd row.
9th row Slip 1, k 7, yo twice, k 2 tog. 11 sts.
11th row As 3rd row.
13th row Slip 1, k 8, yo twice, k 2 tog. 12 sts.
15th row As 3rd row.
16th row P 2 tog, p 1, k to end. 11 sts.
17th row Slip 1, k 6, k 2 tog, yo twice, k 2 tog.
18th row P 2, k to end.

19th row As 3rd row.
20th row P 2 tog, p 1, k to end. 10 sts.
21st row Slip 1, k 5, k 2 tog, yo twice, k 2 tog.
22nd row As 18th row.
23rd row As 3rd row.
24th row P 2 tog, p 1, k to end. 9 sts.
25th row Slip 1, k 4, k 2 tog, yo twice, k 2 tog.
26th row As 18th row.
27th row As 3rd row
28th row P 2 tog, p 1, k to end. 8 sts.
Repeat 1st–28th rows.
Bind off.

 **56** **FLARES**
Directory view, page 28

Skill level: Complex

 Sportweight cotton

Turning rows and some double eyelets add fullness to these lace panels.

METHOD

Note: To prevent a hole when turning to work a short row, wrap the yarn around the next stitch like this: turn, leaving the yarn at the front, slip the first st from the right-hand needle to the left-hand needle, take the yarn to the back, slip the st back onto the right-hand needle, then continue.

Cast on 15 sts.
1st row (WS) K.
2nd row K 12, turn, k to end.
3rd row K.
4th row K 4, [yo, k 2 tog] 4 times, yo twice, k 2 tog, k 1. 16 sts.
5th row K 3, p 1, k 12.

6th row K 5, [yo, k 2 tog] 4 times, yo twice, k 2 tog, k 1. 17 sts.
7th row K 3, p 1, k 13.
8th row K 6, [yo, k 2 tog] 4 times, yo twice, k 2 tog, k 1. 18 sts.
9th row K 3, p 1, k 14.
10th row K.
11th row K 15, turn, k to end.
12th row Bind off 3 sts, k 14. 15 sts.
Repeat 1st–12th rows, ending with an 11th pattern row.
Bind off.

 57 **OYSTER SHELL**
Directory view, page 28

Skill level: Complex

 Sportweight wool

An unusual feature of this edging is the multiple decrease which gathers the stitches into a shell shape.

METHOD

Cast on 16 sts.
1st row (RS) Slip 1, k 2, yo twice, k 13. 18 sts.
2nd row Yo, k 2 tog, k 12, p 1, k 3.
3rd row Slip 1, k to end.
4th row Yo, k 2 tog, k 16.
5th row Slip 1, k 2, yo twice, k 2 tog, yo twice, k 13. 21 sts.
6th row Yo, k 2 tog, k 12, p 1, k 2, p 1, k 3.
7th row As 3rd row.
8th row Yo, k 2 tog, k 19.
9th row Slip 1, k 2, [yo twice, k 2 tog] 3 times, k 12. 24 sts.
10th row Yo, k 2 tog, k 12, p 1, [k 2, p 1] twice, k 3.
11th row As 3rd row.
12th row Yo, k 2 tog, k 22.

13th row Slip 1, k 2, [yo twice, k 2 tog] 4 times, k 13. 28 sts.
14th row Yo, k 2 tog, k 13, p 1, [k 2, p 1] 3 times, k 3.
15th row As 3rd row.
16th row Yo, k 2 tog, k 26.
17th row Slip 1, k 13, slip 1, one at a time slip 10 sts over first 2 sts on left-hand needle, k these 2 sts tog, pass slipped st over, k 1. 16 sts.
18th row Yo, k 2 tog, k 14.
Repeat 1st–18th rows, ending with a 17th pattern row.
Bind off.

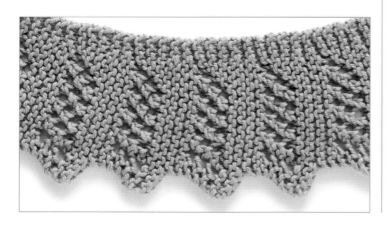

58 CHEVRONS
Directory view, page 28

Skill level: Intermediate

 Sportweight cotton

 Garter stitch emphasizes the wavy lines of this chevron border.

METHOD

Cast on a multiple of 15 sts plus 1.
1st row (RS) K 6, * skpo, k 2 tog, k 11; repeat from *, ending skpo, k 2 tog, k 6.
2nd row K.
3rd row K 1, * m 1, k 4, skpo, k 2 tog, k 4, m 1, k 1; repeat from * to end.
4th row K.
5th row As 3rd row.
6th row K.
7th row K 3, * skpo twice, k 2 tog twice, k 5; repeat from *, ending skpo twice, k 2 tog twice, k 3. Multiple of 9 sts plus 1.
Bind off.

59 HOOPS
Directory view, page 29

Skill level: Easy

 Sportweight cotton

 The fullness of this border means that it lies flat if the top edge is allowed to curve or it flares if the top edge is kept straight.

METHOD

Cast on a multiple of 4 sts.
1st row (RS) K.
2nd row P.
3rd row K.
4th row P.
5th row * K 2 tog, yo twice, skpo; repeat from * to end.
6th row * P 1, (k 1, p 1, k 1, p 1, k 1) in double yo, p 1; repeat from * to end.
7th row K.
Bind off purlwise.

60 FAGGOT AND RIB FLOUNCE
Directory view, page 29

Skill level: Easy

 Sportweight wool

 Both sides of this simple edging are pretty—the faggot stitch is prominent on one side and the rib on the other.

METHOD

Cast on a multiple of 4 sts plus 2.
1st row (WS) K 2, * yo, p 2 tog, k 2; repeat from * to end.
2nd row P 2, * yo, p 2 tog, p 2; repeat from * to end.
Repeat 1st and 2nd rows 7 times.
17th row K 1, * skpo, k 2 tog; repeat from * to last st, k 1.
Bind off purlwise.

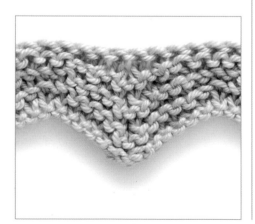

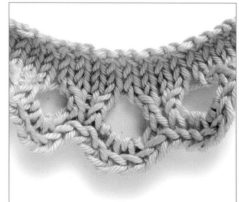

WELTED FLOUNCE
Directory view, page 29

Skill level: Complex

 Sportweight cotton   *Full, chunky flounces edge this elaborate, old-fashioned trim.*

METHOD

Note: Each row has a turned section and is in effect a double row. All sts should be slipped knitwise.

Cast on 15 sts.
1st row K 3, [yo, k 2 tog] twice, yo, [k 8, turn, sl 1, p 7, turn] twice, k 8, turn, slip 1, p 7, k 8. 16 sts.
2nd row K 4, [yo, k 2 tog] twice, yo, [p 8, turn, slip 1, k 7, turn] twice, p 8, turn, slip 1, k 16. 17 sts.
3rd row K 5, [yo, k 2 tog] twice, yo, [k 8, turn, slip 1, p 7, turn] twice, k 8, turn, slip 1, p 7, k 10. 18 sts.
4th row K 6, [yo, k 2 tog] twice, yo, [p 8, turn, slip 1, k 7, turn] twice, p 8, turn, slip 1, k 18. 19 sts.
5th row K 7, [yo, k 2 tog] twice, yo, [k 8, turn, slip 1, p 7, turn] twice, k 8, turn, slip 1, p 7, k 12. 20 sts.
6th row K 8, [yo, k 2 tog] twice, yo, [p 8, turn, slip 1, k 7, turn] twice, p 8, turn, slip 1, k 20. 21 sts.
7th row K 9, [yo, k 2 tog] twice, yo, [k 8, turn, slip 1, p 7, turn] twice, k 8, turn, sl 1, p 7, k 14. 22 sts.
8th row K 10, [yo, k 2 tog] twice, yo, [p 8, turn, slip 1, k 7, turn] twice, p 8, turn, slip 1, k 22. 23 sts.
9th row K 8, [k 2 tog, yo] 3 times, k 2 tog, k 7, [turn, slip 1, p 7, turn, k 8] twice, turn, slip 1, p 7, k 14. 22 sts.
10th row K 7, [k 2 tog, yo] 3 times, p 2 tog, p 7, [turn, slip 1, k 7, turn, p 8] twice, turn, slip 1, k 20. 21 sts.
11th row K 6, [k 2 tog, yo] 3 times, k 2 tog, k 7, [turn, slip 1, p 7, turn, k 8] twice, turn, slip 1, p 7, k 12. 20 sts.
12th row K 5, [k 2 tog, yo] 3 times, p 2 tog, p 7, [turn, slip 1, k 7, turn, p 8] twice, turn, slip 1, k 18. 19 sts.
13th row K 4, [k 2 tog, yo] 3 times, k 2 tog, k 7, [turn, slip 1, p 7, turn, k 8] twice, turn, slip 1, p 7, k 10. 18 sts.
14th row K 3, [k 2 tog, yo] 3 times, p 2 tog, p 7, [turn, slip 1, k 7, turn, p 8] twice, turn, slip 1, k 16. 17 sts.
15th row K 2, [k 2 tog, yo] 3 times, k 2 tog, k 7, [turn, slip 1, p 7, turn, k 8] twice, slip 1, p 7, k 8. 16 sts.
16th row K 1, [k 2 tog, yo] 3 times, p 2 tog, p 7, [turn, slip 1, k 7, turn, p 8] twice, turn, slip 1, k 14. 15 sts.
Repeat 1st–16th rows.
Bind off.

 LOOP-EDGED FRILL
Directory view, page 30

Skill level: Intermediate

 2 ply Jumper Weight Shetland wool  *Turning rows give this frill its fullness, so it flares if used along a straight edge but lies flat if joined into a circle.*

METHOD

Note: The 3rd row contains a turned section and so is in effect two rows.

Cast on 8 sts.
1st row (RS) [Yo, k 2 tog] twice, k 4.
2nd row K 2, p 6.
3rd row [Yo, k 2 tog] twice, k 2, bring yarn to front, slip first st from left-hand needle to right-hand needle, take yarn to back, slip st back on to left-hand needle, turn, p 6.
Repeat 1st–3rd rows, ending with a 1st or 3rd row.
Bind off.

63 BELL RUFFLE
Directory view, page 30

Skill level: Intermediate

 Sportweight wool

 Central double decreases shape each bell in this firm little ruffle.

METHOD

Note: s2kpo—slip 2 sts as if to k 2 tog, k 1, pass slipped sts over.

Cast on a multiple of 10 sts plus 3.
1st row (RS) P.
2nd row K 3, * p 7, k 3; repeat from * to end.
3rd row P 3, * k 7, p 3; repeat from * to end.
4th row As 2nd row.
5th row P 3, * k 2, s2kpo, k 2, p 3; repeat from * to end.
6th row K 3, * p 5, k 3; repeat from * to end.
7th row P 3, * k 1, s2kpo, k 1, p 3; repeat from * to end.
8th row K 3, * p 3, k 3; repeat from * to end.
9th row P 3, * s2kpo, p 3; repeat from * to end.
10th row K.
Bind off purlwise.

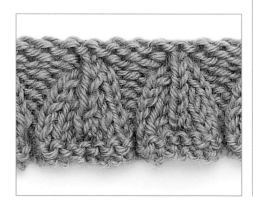

64 RIBBED PLEATS
Directory view, page 30

Skill level: Easy

 Worsted wool
Two sizes of knitting needles

 This versatile stitch has almost the same appearance on both sides.

METHOD

Cast on a multiple of 8 sts plus 4.
1st row (RS) K 4, * p 4, k 4; repeat from * to end.
2nd row P 4, * k 4, p 4; repeat from * to end.
Repeat these 2 rows once more.
Change to one size smaller needles.
5th row Skpo, k 2 tog, * p 2 tog, p 2 tog tbl, skpo, k 2 tog; repeat from * to end.
Multiple of 4 sts plus 2.
P 2 rows.
Bind off.

65 MOCK PLEATS
Directory view, page 30

Skill level: Easy

 *Worsted cotton*
Two sizes of knitting needles

This simple stitch exploits the tendency of vertical knit and purl stitches to fold into a rib.

METHOD

Cast on a multiple of 5 sts.
1st row (RS) * K 4, p 1; repeat from * to end.
2nd row * K 2, p 3; repeat from * to end.
3rd row As 2nd row.
4th row * K 4, p 1; repeat from * to end.
5th row As 2nd row.
6th row As 2nd row.
7th row As 1st row.
Change to smaller size needles.
8th row * P 2 tog, p 3; repeat from * to end.
Multiple of 4 sts.
9th row P.
Bind off.

66 LADDER FRILL

Directory view, page 31

Skill level: Intermediate

 *2 ply
Jumper Weight
Shetland wool*

 *The cobweb nature
of this frill is achieved
with dropped rib
stitches and the use
of a fine, springy yarn.*

METHOD

Cast on a multiple of 3 sts plus 1.
1st row (RS) K 1 tbl, * p 2, k 1 tbl; repeat
from * to end.
2nd row P 1 tbl, * k 1 tbl, k 1, p 1 tbl;
repeat from * to end.
Repeat 1st and 2nd rows twice.
7th row K 1 tbl, * drop next st off needle,
p 1 tbl, k 1 tbl; repeat from * to end.
8th row P 1 tbl, * k 1, p 1 tbl; repeat from *
to end.
9th row K 1 tbl, * p 1, k 1 tbl; repeat from *
to end.
10th row As 8th row.
Bind off in rib.
Unravel the dropped sts down all the rows.

67 WELTED RUFFLE

Directory view, page 31

Skill level: Intermediate

 Worsted cotton

 *Sideways-knitted welts
have turning rows built
in so that they appear
to be gathered along
one edge.*

METHOD

Cast on 9 sts.
1st row (WS) Slip 1, k 8.
2nd row P 6, turn, slip 1, k 5.
3rd row P 6, k 3.
4th row Slip 1, k 2, p 6.
5th row K 6, turn, slip 1 purlwise, p 5.
6th row K 9.
Repeat 1st–6th rows.
Bind off.

68 FEATHER AND FAN

Directory view, page 31

Skill level: Intermediate

 *Sportweight
cotton*

 *A traditional Shetland
lace stitch has been
adapted to make an
attractive border.*

METHOD

Cast on a multiple of 17 sts.
1st row (RS) K.
2nd row P.
3rd row * K 2 tog 3 times, [yo, k 1] 5 times,
yo, k 2 tog 3 times; repeat from * to end.
4th row K.
Repeat 1st–4th rows once more, then repeat
1st and 2nd rows again.
Decrease row (RS) * K 3, [k 2 tog twice, k 3]
twice; repeat from * to end.
Bind off.

LACY EDGINGS

SEE ALSO

Knitting abbreviations, page 9
Refresher course, pages 10–13

Directory view, page 32

69 BUNTING

Directory view, page 32

Skill level: Intermediate

 Sportweight wool

 These small lacy triangles are neat and very well-defined.

METHOD

Note: sk2po—slip one st knitwise, k 2 tog, pass slipped st over.

Cast on 4 sts.
1st row (RS) Slip 1, k 1, yo twice, k 2. 6 sts.
2nd row K 3, p 1, k 2.
3rd row Slip 1, k 5.
4th row K 6.
5th row Slip 1, k 1, [yo twice, k 2 tog] twice. 8 sts.
6th row [K 2, p 1] twice, k 2.
7th row Slip 1, k 7.
8th row K 8.
9th row Slip 1, k 1, [yo twice, k 2 tog] 3 times. 11 sts.
10th row [K 2, p 1] 3 times, k 2.
11th row Slip 1, k 10.
12th row K 11.
13th row Slip 1, k 1, [yo twice, k 2 tog] 3 times, yo twice, sk2po. 14 sts.
14th row [K 2, p 1] 4 times, k 2.
15th row Slip 1, k 13.
16th row Bind off 10 sts, k 3. 4 sts.
Repeat 1st–16th rows.
Bind off.

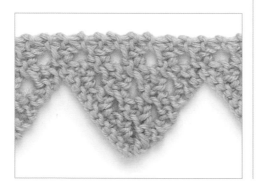

70 MINI LACE

Skill level: Easy

 Worsted cotton

 This is a neat little edging that's not unlike Baby Lace (see page 85).

METHOD

Cast on 6 sts.
1st row (RS) Yo, k 2 tog, k 4.
2nd row Slip 1, k 3, yo twice, k 2 tog. 7 sts.
3rd row Yo, k 2 tog, p 1, k 1, k 2 tog, k 1. 6 sts.
4th row Slip 1, k 5.
Repeat 1st–4th rows.
Bind off.

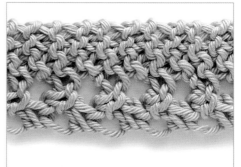

71 SHORELINE
Directory view, page 33

Skill level: Complex

  Sportweight wool · Waves and foam can easily be read into the smooth curves of this design.

METHOD

Note: ssk2po—slip 2 sts one at a time knitwise, insert left-hand needle in the fronts of these sts, k 2 tog, slip resulting st onto left-hand needle, slip next st over it then slip it back onto right-hand needle.

Cast on 14 sts.
1st row (RS) Slip 1, k 4, yo, k 5, yo, k 2 tog, yo, k 2. 16 sts.
2nd and WS rows K 2, p to last 2 sts, p 2.
3rd row Slip 1, k 5, ssk2po, k 2, [yo, k 2 tog] twice, k 1. 14 sts.
5th row Slip 1, k 4, k 2 tog, k 2, [yo, k 2 tog] twice, k 1. 13 sts.
7th row Slip 1, k 3, k 2 tog, k 2, [yo, k 2 tog] twice, k 1. 12 sts.

9th row Slip 1, k 2, k 2 tog, k 2, [yo, k 2 tog] twice, k 1. 11 sts.
11th row Slip 1, k 1, k 2 tog, k 2, yo, k 1, yo, k 2 tog, yo, k 2. 12 sts.
13th row Slip 1, k 4, yo, k 3, yo, k 2 tog, yo, k 2. 14 sts.
14th row As 2nd row.
Repeat 1st–14th rows, ending with a 1st pattern row.
Bind off in pattern.

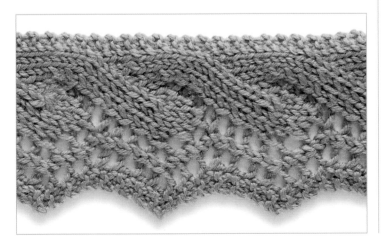

72 ZIGZAG
Directory view, page 33

Skill level: Intermediate

  Sportweight wool · Very strongly defined diagonals give this lace its name.

METHOD

Cast on 7 sts.
1st row (RS) K 3, yo, skpo, yo, k 2. 8 sts.
2nd, 4th 6th, 8th, 10th, 12th, and 14th rows Slip 1, p to last 2 sts, k 2.
3rd row K 4, yo, skpo, yo k 2. 9 sts.
5th row K 5, yo skpo, yo, k 2. 10 sts.
7th row K 6, yo, skpo, yo, k2. 11 sts.
9th row K 7, yo, skpo, yo, k 2. 12 sts.
11th row K 8, yo, skpo, yo, k 2. 13 sts.
13th row K 9, yo, skpo, yo, k2. 14 sts.

15th row K 10, yo, skpo, k 2. 15 sts.
16th row Bind off 8 sts, p 4, k 2. 7 sts.
Repeat 1st–16th rows, ending with a 15th pattern row.
Bind off in pattern.

73 TREFOIL
Directory view, page 33

Skill level: Easy

 Worsted wool

 A very regular zigzag garter stitch edging is dotted with eyelets in groups of three.

METHOD

Cast on 5 sts.
1st row (RS) K 3, yo twice, k 2. 7 sts.
2nd row K 3, p 1, k 3.
3rd and 4th rows K.
5th row K 3, yo twice, k 2 tog, yo twice, k 2. 10 sts.
6th row K 3, p 1, k 2, p 1, k 3.
7th row K.
8th row Bind off 5 sts, k 4. 5 sts.
Repeat 1st–8th rows.
Bind off.

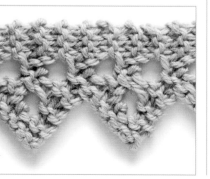

74 FLORAL SCALLOPS
Directory view, page 34

Skill level: Complex

2 ply Jumper Weight Shetland wool

 This stitch pattern is a little idiosyncratic as the double yarn-over increases are not always made on right-side rows.

METHOD

Note: b1—make bobble: (k 1, p 1, k 1, p 1, k 1) in next st, turn, k 5, turn, slip 2nd, 3rd, 4th, and 5th sts over first, k this st tbl; s2kpo—slip 2 sts as if to k 2 tog, k 1, pass slipped sts over.

Cast on 8 sts.
1st row (RS) Slip 1, k 7.
2nd row K 8.
3rd row Slip 1, k 3, yo twice, k 2 tog, yo twice, k 2. 11 sts.
4th row K 2, p 1, k 3, p 1, k 4.
5th row Slip 1, k 10.
6th row K 2, yo twice, skpo, k 1, k 2 tog, yo twice, skpo, k 2. 12 sts.
7th row Slip 1, k 2, p 1, k 2, b1, k 2, p 1, k 2.
8th row K 12.
9th row Slip 1, k 2, k 2 tog, yo twice, s2kpo, yo twice, k 2 tog twice. 11 sts.
10th row K 2, p 1, k 3, p 1, k 4.
11th row Slip 1, k 10.
12th row Slipping first st, bind off 3 sts, k 7. 8 sts. Repeat 1st–12th rows.
Bind off.

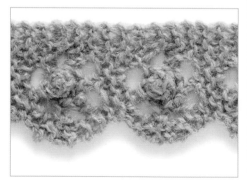

75 ASPEN LEAF
Directory view, page 34

Skill level: Intermediate

2 ply Jumper Weight Shetland wool

 Although the edge is shaped, this leafy design has the same number of stitches on every row.

METHOD

Cast on 12 sts.
1st row (WS) Slip 1, k 1, p 10.
2nd row Yo, k 1, yo, k 2, skpo, k 2 tog, k 2, yo, k 2 tog, k 1.
3rd row As 1st row.
4th row Yo, k 3, yo, k 1, skpo, k 2 tog, k 1, yo, k 2 tog, k 1.
5th row As 1st row.
6th row Yo, k 5, yo, skpo, k 2 tog, yo, k 2 tog, k 1.
7th row As 1st row.
8th row Yo, k 3, skpo, k 2, [yo, k 2 tog] twice, k 1.
Repeat 1st–8th rows.
Bind off.

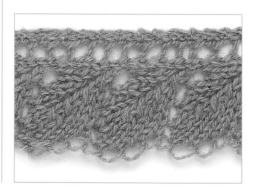

76 BABY LACE

Directory view, page 34

Skill level: Intermediate

 *2 ply
Jumper Weight
Shetland wool*

 *This is a subtle lace
which looks pretty in
almost any yarn.*

METHOD

Cast on 5 sts.
1st row (RS) Slip 1, k 2, yo twice, p 2 tog.
6 sts.
2nd row Yo, k 2, p 1, k 3. 7 sts.
3rd row Slip 1, k 2, p 4.
4th row Slipping first st, bind off 2 sts,
k 4. 5 sts.
Repeat 1st–4th rows.
Bind off.

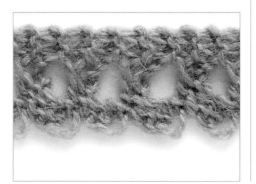

77 POINTS AND BEADS

Directory view, page 34

Skill level: Intermediate

 *2 ply
Jumper Weight
Shetland wool*

 *Starting alternate
rows with a yarn-over
loop makes a
delicate heading.*

METHOD

*Note: To make this yarn-over at the beginning
of a row bring yarn forward underneath the
right-hand needle, take it over the needle and
to the front, ready to p 2 tog.*

Cast on 6 sts.
1st row (RS) Yo, p 2 tog, k 2, yo, k 2. 7 sts.
2nd row P 5, yo, p 2 tog.
3rd row Yo, p 2 tog, k 2, yo, k 1, yo, k 2. 9 sts.
4th row P 7, yo, p 2 tog.
5th row Yo, p 2 tog, k 2, [yo, k 1] 3 times,
yo, k 2. 13 sts.
6th row Bind off 7 sts purlwise, p 3, yo,
p 2 tog. 6 sts.
Repeat 1st–6th rows.
Bind off.

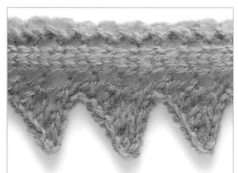

78 TRELLIS

Directory view, page 35

Skill level: Intermediate

 *Sportweight
cotton*

 *Diagonal lines of
decreases add texture
to this openwork.*

METHOD

Cast on 7 sts.
1st row (WS) K 1, [yo, k 2 tog] twice, yo, k 2.
8 sts.
2nd, 4th, 6th, 8th, 10th, and 12th rows K.
3rd row K 2, [yo, k 2 tog] twice, yo, k 2. 9 sts.
5th row K 3, [yo, k 2 tog] twice, yo, k 2.
10 sts.
7th row K 4, [yo, k 2 tog] 3 times.
9th row K 3, [yo, k 2 tog] twice, yo, k 3 tog.
9 sts.
11th row K 2, [yo, k 2 tog] twice, yo, k 3 tog.
8 sts.
13th row K 1, [yo, k 2 tog] twice, yo, k 3 tog.
7 sts.
14th row Kfb, k to end. 8 sts.
Repeat 3rd–14th rows, ending with a
13th pattern row.
Bind off.

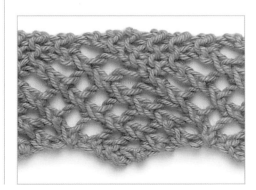

79 LIME LEAF
Directory view, page 35

Skill level: Complex

 Sportweight cotton

 Although this lace has a wavy edge the stitch count remains the same on every row.

METHOD

Note: Slip 1 p—slip one st purlwise with yarn at back; sk2po—slip one st knitwise, k 2 tog, pass slipped st over.

Cast on 13 sts.
1st row (RS) Slip 1 p, sk2po, yo, k 5, yo, k 1 tbl, yo, skpo, k 1.
2nd, 4th, 6th, and 8th rows Slip 1 p, p 11, k 1 tbl.
3rd row Slip 1 p, k 1 tbl, yo, k 1, k 2 tog tbl, p 1, skpo, k 1, yo, k 1 tbl, yo, skpo, k 1.
5th row As 3rd row.
7th row Slip 1 p, skpo, yo, k 2 tog tbl, p 1, skpo, yo, [k 1 tbl, yo] twice, skpo, k 1.
9th row Slip 1 p, skpo, yo, k 3 tog tbl, yo, k 3, yo, k 1 tbl, yo, skpo, k 1.
10th row As 2nd row.
Repeat 1st–10th rows.
Bind off.

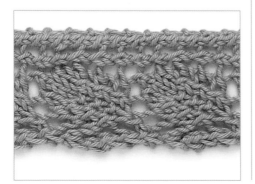

80 FALLING LEAF
Directory view, page 35

Skill level: Complex

 Sportweight cotton

 Curving leaves and stems are well defined against a reverse stocking stitch background.

METHOD

Cast on 6 sts.
1st row (RS) K 1, p 1, k 1, [yo, k 1] twice, p 1. 8 sts.
2nd row K 1, p 5, k 2.
3rd row K 1, p 1, m1p, k 2, yo, k 1, yo, k 2, p 1. 11 sts.
4th row K 1, p 7, k 3.
5th row K 1, p 2, m1p, k 3, yo, k 1, yo, k 3, p 1. 14 sts.
6th row K 1, p 9, k 4.
7th row K 1, p 3, m1p, skpo, k 5, k 2 tog, p 1. 13 sts.
8th row K 1, p 7, k 5.
9th row K 1, p 2, k 1, p 1, m1p, skpo, k 3, k 2 tog, p 1. 12 sts.
10th row K 1, p 5, k 2, p 1, k 3.
11th row [K 1, p 2] twice, m1p, skpo, k 1, k 2 tog, p 1. 11 sts.
12th row K 1, p 3, k 3, p 1, k 3.
13th row K 1, p 2, k 1, p 3, m1p, sk2po, p 1. 10 sts.
14th row Slipping first st, bind off 4 sts, k 1, p 1, k 3. 6 sts.
Repeat 1st–14th rows.
Bind off.

81 CINQUEFOIL
Directory view, page 35

Skill level: Intermediate

 Sportweight wool

 This is an old-fashioned garter stitch lace with regular, defined points.

METHOD

Cast on 8 sts.
1st row (RS) Slip 1, k 2, [yo twice, k 2 tog] twice, k 1. 10 sts.
2nd row K 3, p 1, k 2, p 1, k 3.
3rd row Slip 1, k 9.
4th row K 10.
5th row Slip 1, k 2, [yo twice, k 2 tog] 3 times, k 1. 13 sts.
6th row K 3, p 1, [k 2, p 1] twice, k 3.
7th row Slip 1, k 12.
8th row K 13.
9th row Slip 1, k 12.
10th row Bind off 5 sts, k 7. 8 sts.
Repeat 1st–10th rows.
Bind off.

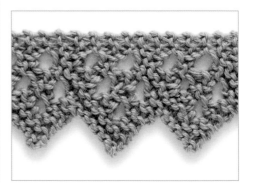

82 TEXTURED DIAMONDS

Directory view, page 36

Skill level: Complex

 Sportweight cotton
Cable needle

 This garter stitch lace has the addition of knops made by wrapping the yarn around groups of stitches.

METHOD

Note: sk2po—slip 1 st knitwise, k2tog, pass slipped st over.

Cast on 11 sts.
1st row (RS) Slip 1, k 4, skpo, yo, skpo, k 2. 10 sts.
2nd row Yo, k 3, p 1, k 6. 11 sts.
3rd row Slip 1, k 3, skpo, [yo twice, skpo] twice, k 1. 12 sts.
4th row Yo, k 3, p 1, k 2, p 1, k 5. 13 sts.
5th row Slip 1, k 2, skpo, yo twice, skpo, k 1, k 2 tog, yo twice, skpo, k 1.
6th row Yo, k 3, [p 1, k 4] twice. 14 sts.
7th row Slip 1, k 1, skpo, yo twice, skpo, make knop: slip next 3 sts onto cable needle and hold at the front, take yarn around these sts 3 times in a counterclockwise direction so

that the yarn finishes at the back, slip these 3 sts onto right-hand needle; k 2 tog, yo twice, skpo, k 1.
8th row K 2 tog, k 1, p 1, k 6, p 1, k 3. 13 sts.
9th row Slip 1, k 2, skpo, yo twice, skpo, k 1, k 2 tog, yo twice, skpo, k 1.
10th row K 2 tog, k 1, [p 1, k 4] twice. 12 sts.
11th row Slip 1, k 3, skpo, yo twice, sk2po, yo twice, skpo, k 1.
12th row K 2 tog, k 1, p 1, k 2, p 1, k 5. 11 sts.
Repeat 1st–12th rows, ending with a 1st pattern row.
Bind off.

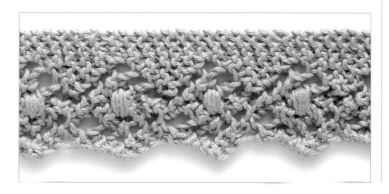

83 CHEVRON LACE

Directory view, page 36

Skill level: Intermediate

 Sportweight cotton

 There's something very satisfying about the symmetry of these chevrons.

METHOD

Note: s2kpo—slip 2 stitches as if to k 2 tog, k 1, pass slipped stitches over.

Cast on 11 sts.
1st row (WS) P.
2nd row Slip 1, k 1, yo, k 2 tog, yo, s2kpo, yo, k 2 tog, yo, k 2.
3rd and WS rows P.
4th row Slip 1, k 1, [yo, k 2 tog] twice, k 1, yo, skpo, yo, k 2. 12 sts.
6th row Slip 1, k 1, [yo, k 2 tog] twice, k 2, yo, skpo, yo, k 2. 13 sts.
8th row Slip 1, k 1, [yo, k 2 tog] twice, k 3, yo, skpo, yo, k 2. 14 sts.
10th row Slip 1, k 1, [yo, k 2 tog] twice, k 4, yo, skpo, yo, k 2. 15 sts.
12th row Slip 1, k 1, [yo, k 2 tog] twice, k 2, skpo, [yo, k 2 tog] twice, k 1. 14 sts.
14th row Slip 1, k 1, [yo, k 2 tog] twice, k 1, skpo, [yo, k 2 tog] twice, k 1. 13 sts.

16th row Slip 1, k 1, [yo, k 2 tog] twice, skpo, [yo, k 2 tog] twice, k 1. 12 sts.
18th row Slip 1, k 1, yo, k 2 tog, s2kpo, [yo, k 2 tog] twice, k 1. 11 sts.
19th row P.
Repeat 4th–19th rows.
Bind off.

84 DOTS AND DASHES

Directory view, page 36

Skill level: Intermediate

 Sportweight cotton

 Diagonal grouping makes a pretty lace with simple ingredients.

METHOD

Cast on 12 sts.
1st row (RS) Slip 1, k 1, yo, k 2 tog, k 3, yo, k 2 tog, yo twice, k 2 tog, k 1. 13 sts.
2nd row K 3, p 1, k 9.
3rd row Slip 1, k 2, yo, k 2 tog, k 3, yo, k 2 tog, yo twice, k 2 tog, k 1. 14 sts.
4th row K 3, p 1, k 10.
5th row Slip 1, [k 3, yo, k 2 tog] twice, yo twice, k 2 tog, k 1. 15 sts.
6th row K 3, p 1, k 11.
7th row Slip 1, k 14.
8th row Bind off 3 sts, k 11. 12 sts.
Repeat 1st–8th rows.
Bind off.

85 FISH EYE

Directory view, page 37

Skill level: Intermediate

 Worsted cotton

 Even in a solid yarn this lacy garter stitch trim remains bold and well-defined.

METHOD

Cast on 5 sts.
1st row (RS) K 2, yo, k 3. 6 sts.
2nd row K 6.
3rd row K 2, yo, k 4. 7 sts.
4th row K 7.
5th row K 2, yo, k 1, k 2 tog, yo 3 times, k 2. 10 sts.
6th row K 2, (k 1, p 1, k 1) in triple yo, k 5.
7th row K 2, yo, k 8. 11 sts.
8th row Bind off 6 sts, k 4. 5 sts.
Repeat 1st–8th rows.
Bind off.

86 BLACKBERRY LACE

Directory view, page 37

Skill level: Complex

 Sportweight wool

 Although it's only a four-row repeat this lace is densely patterned on every row.

METHOD

Note: kfb—k in front and back of st; sk2po—slip one st knitwise, k 2 tog, pass slipped st over.

Cast on 17 sts.
1st row (WS) Slip 1, k 1, [yo, k 2 tog, k 1] twice, k 2 tog, yo, k 1, yo, k 2 tog, k 1, k 2 tog, yo, kfb. 18 sts.
2nd row [K 3, yo, sk2po, yo] twice, k 6.
3rd row Slip 1, k 1, [yo, k 2 tog, k 1, k 2 tog, yo, k 1] twice, yo, k 3, kfb. 20 sts.
4th row Bind off 4 sts, yo, k 3, yo, sk2po, yo, k 3, yo, k 2 tog, k 4. 17 sts.
Repeat 1st–4th rows.
Bind off.

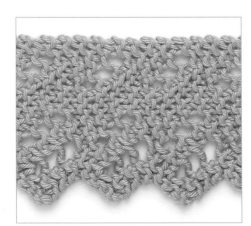

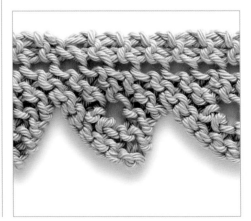

87 CLASSIC
Directory view, page 37

Skill level: Intermediate

 Sportweight wool   *Double yarn-overs shape this quite austere lace.*

METHOD

Cast on 7 sts.
1st row (RS) K 2, yo, skpo, k 1, yo twice, skpo. 8 sts.
2nd, 4th, 6th, 8th, and 10th rows P 1, k 1, p to last 4 sts, yo, p 2 tog, k 2.
3rd row K 2, yo, skpo, k 2, yo twice, skpo. 9 sts.
5th row K 2, yo, skpo, k 3, yo twice, skpo. 10 sts.
7th row K 2, yo, skpo, k 4, yo twice, skpo. 11 sts.
9th row K 2, yo, skpo, k 5, yo twice, skpo. 12 sts.

11th row K 2, yo, skpo, k to last 2 sts, k 2 tog. 11 sts.
12th, 14th, 16th, and 18th rows P to last 4 sts, yo, p 2 tog, k 2.
13th row As 11th row. 10 sts.
15th row As 11th row. 9 sts.
17th row As 11th row. 8 sts.
19th row As 11th row. 7 sts.
20th row As 12th row.
Repeat 1st–20th rows.
Bind off.

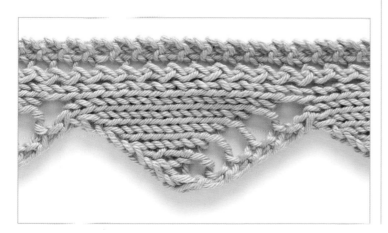

---

88 LEAF AND BERRY
Directory view, page 38

Skill level: Complex

 Sportweight wool *This design isn't too daunting for a competent knitter as the repeat is only eight rows long.*

METHOD

Note: sk2po—slip 1, k 2 tog, pass slipped st over; ssk2po—slip 2 sts one at a time knitwise, insert left-hand needle in the fronts of these sts, k 2 tog, slip resulting st onto left-hand needle, slip next st over it then slip it back onto right-hand needle.

Cast on 12 sts.
1st row (RS) K 1, k 2 tog, yo twice, skpo, yo, k 1, yo, (k 1, p 1, k 1) in next st, [yo, k 1] twice, yo twice, k 2 tog, k 1. 19 sts.
2nd row K 3, p 1, k 1, p 9, k 2, p 1, k 2.
3rd row K 1, k 2 tog, yo twice, skpo, [yo, k 3] 3 times, yo, [k 1, yo twice] twice,

k 2 tog, k 1. 26 sts.
4th row K 3, p 1, k 2, p 1, k 1, p 5, p 3 tog, p 5, k 2, p 1, k 2. 24 sts.
5th row K 1, k 2 tog, yo twice, skpo, [yo, skpo, k 1, k 2 tog, yo, k 1] twice, [yo twice, k 2 tog] 3 times, k 1. 27 sts.
6th row K 3, [p 1, k 2] twice, p 1, k 1, [p 2 tog, p 1] 3 times, p 2 tog, k 2, p 1, k 2. 23 sts.
7th row K 1, k 2 tog, yo twice, skpo, yo, sk2po, k 1, ssk2po, k 11. 20 sts.
8th row Slipping first st, bind off 6 sts, k 4, p 3 tog, k 3, p 1, k 2. 12 sts.
Repeat 1st–8th rows.
Bind off.

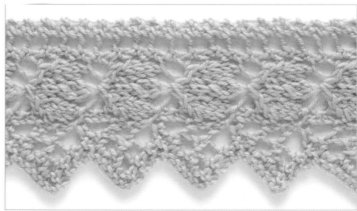

89 PENNANTS
Directory view, page 38

Skill level: Intermediate

 Sportweight wool

 Diagonal eyelets shape and decorate this mainly stocking stitch edging.

METHOD

Cast on 4 sts.
1st row (RS) K 1, yo, k 1, p 1, k 1. 5 sts.
2nd and WS rows K 2, p to end.
3rd row K 1, yo, k 2, p 1, k 1. 6 sts.
5th row K 1, yo, k 1, k 2 tog, yo, p 1, k 1. 7 sts.
7th row K 1, yo, k 1, k 2 tog, yo, k 1, p 1, k 1. 8 sts.
9th row K 1, yo, k 1, k 2 tog, yo, k 2, p 1, k 1. 9 sts.
11th row K 1, yo, [k 1, k 2 tog, yo] twice, p 1, k 1. 10 sts.
13th row K 1, yo, [k 1, k 2 tog, yo] twice, k 1, p 1, k 1. 11 sts.
15th row K 1, yo, [k 1, k 2 tog, yo] twice, k 2, p 1, k 1. 12 sts.

17th row K 1, yo, [k 1, k 2 tog, yo] 3 times, p 1, k 1. 13 sts.
19th row Loosely bind off 9 sts, yo, k 1, p 1, k 1. 5 sts. Repeat 2nd–19th rows.
Bind off in pattern.

 90 FERN LEAF
Directory view, page 38

Skill level: Complex

 2 ply Jumper Weight Shetland wool

This is one of many graceful leafy lace edgings from the past—the instructions are repetitive rather than difficult.

METHOD

Cast on 14 sts.
1st row (RS) Slip 1, k 2, [yo, k 2 tog] twice, k 1, yo twice, k 2 tog twice, yo, k 2. 15 sts.
2nd row K 5, (k 1, p 1, k 1, p 1) in double yo, k 8. 17 sts.
3rd row Slip 1, k 3, [yo, k 2 tog] twice, k 5, k 2 tog, yo, k 2.
4th and WS rows K.
5th row Slip 1, k 4, [yo, k 2 tog] twice, k 4, k 2 tog, yo, k 2.
7th row Slip 1, k 5, [yo, k 2 tog] twice, k 3, k 2 tog, yo, k 2.
9th row Slip 1, k 6, [yo, k 2 tog] twice, k 2, k 2 tog, yo, k 2.
11th row Slip 1, k 7, [yo, k 2 tog] twice, k 1, k 2 tog, yo, k 2.
13th row Slip 1, k 8, [yo, k 2 tog] twice, k 2 tog, yo, k 2.
15th row Slip 1, k 9, [yo, k 2 tog] twice, k 1, yo, k 2. 18 sts.

17th row Slip 1, k 10, yo, k 2 tog twice, sl last st back onto left-hand needle, sl next 3 sts, one at a time over it then replace st on right-hand needle. 14 sts.
18th row K.
Repeat 1st–18th rows, ending with a 17th pattern row.
Bind off.

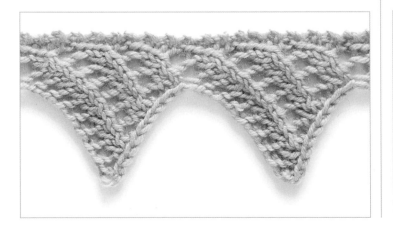

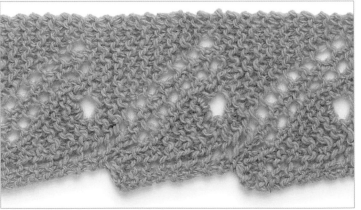

PICOT LACE
Directory view, page 39

Skill level: Intermediate

2 ply
Jumper Weight
Shetland wool

As this design shows, a simple pattern repeat can make an intricate-looking stitch.

METHOD

Cast on 7 sts.
1st row (RS) K 1, k 2 tog, yo, k 2, yo twice, k 1, yo 3 times, k 1. 12 sts.
2nd row K 2, p 1, k 3, p 1, k 2, p 1, k 2.
3rd row K 1, k 2 tog, yo, k 2, skpo, k 5. 11 sts.
4th row Bind off 4 sts, k 3, p 1, k 2. 7 sts.
Repeat 1st–4th rows, ending with a 3rd pattern row.
Bind off.

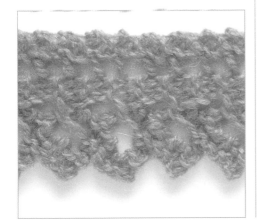

 ## SHARK'S TOOTH
Directory view, page 39

Skill level: Easy

2 ply
Jumper Weight
Shetland wool

A yarn-over increase on every row makes long, narrow points.

METHOD

Cast on 5 sts.
1st row (RS) Slip 1, k 2, yo, k 2. 6 sts.
2nd row K 2, yo, k 4. 7 sts.
3rd row Slip 1, k 4, yo, k 2. 8 sts.
4th row K 2, yo, k 6. 9 sts.
5th row Slip 1, k 6, yo, k 2. 10 sts.
6th row K 2, yo, k 8. 11 sts.
7th row Slip 1, k 8, yo, k 2. 12 sts.
8th row K 2, yo, k 10. 13 sts.
9th row Slip 1, k 10, yo, k 2. 14 sts.
10th row Bind off 9 sts, k 4. 5 sts.
Repeat 1st–10th rows.
Bind off.

 ## WILLOW LEAF
Directory view, page 39

Skill level: Intermediate

2 ply
Jumper Weight
Shetland wool

Pairs of double yarn-overs create these softly trailing leaf shapes in garter stitch.

METHOD

Cast on 6 sts.
1st row (RS) K.
2nd row K 2 tog, yo twice, k 2 tog, yo twice, k 2. 8 sts.
3rd, 5th, 7th, and 9th rows K, working (k 1, p 1) in each double yo.
4th row K 2 tog, yo twice, k 2 tog, yo twice, k 4. 10 sts.
6th row K 2 tog, yo twice, k 2 tog, yo twice, k 6. 12 sts.
8th row K 2 tog, yo twice, k 2 tog, yo twice, k 8. 14 sts.
10th row Cast off 8 sts, k 5. 6 sts.
Repeat 1st–10th rows.
Bind off.

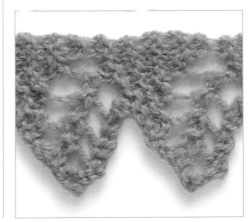

LOOPS AND FRINGES

SEE ALSO

Knitting abbreviations, page 9
Refresher course, pages 10–13

 94 PICOT LOOPS
Directory view, page 40

Skill level: Intermediate

 Sportweight cotton

 Joining a length of three picots on a subsequent row makes a neat loop looking like a little clover leaf.

METHOD

Note: To cast on 2 sts on 5th row: k in next st but do not slip it off, transfer new st from right-hand to left-hand needle then work the next st in the same way.

Cast on 4 sts.
1st row (RS) Slip 1, k 3.
2nd, 3rd, and 4th rows As first row.
5th row Slip 1, k 2, [cast on 2 sts as above, bind off 2 sts, slip st from right-hand needle to left-hand needle] 3 times, bring yarn to front, slip nearest st from right-hand needle to left-hand needle, take yarn to back, slip st back on to right-hand needle, k 1 tbl.
6th–10th rows Slip 1, k 3.
Repeat 1st–10th rows.
Bind off.

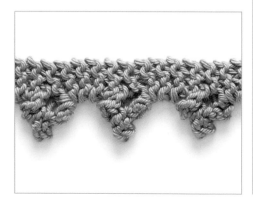

95 SEQUIN-TIED FRINGE
Directory view, page 40

Skill level: Easy

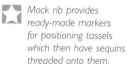 *Sportweight cotton*
Crochet hook

Sequins, sewing needle, and strong thread

 Mock rib provides ready-made markers for positioning tassels which then have sequins threaded onto them.

METHOD

Cast on a multiple of 4 sts plus 2.
1st row (RS) K.
2nd row K 2, * p 2, k 2; repeat from * to end.
Repeat these 2 rows once more, then work 1st row again.
Bind off.

Tassels

For each tassel cut 4 strands of yarn, approximately 4¾ in (12 cm) long. Double the strands, insert crochet hook from wrong side in a rib and pull a loop through (see page 12 for illustration). Insert hook in loop and pull ends through. Tighten the knot. Use sewing needle to thread sequins randomly, tying each one in position (see page 13 for sequin-threading). Trim ends of tassels.

96 GARTER STITCH LOOPS

Directory view, page 41

Skill level: Intermediate

 Worsted wool

 This is simply a garter stitch fringe caught up after a few rows to form loops.

METHOD

Cast on 4 sts
1st row (RS) Slip 1, k 3.
2nd row Slip 1, k 3.
3rd row Cast on one st by working k in the next st without slipping it off, transfer the new st from the right-hand to the left-hand needle; inserting the needle between the first 2 sts on left-hand needle each time, cast on 6 more sts in this way, making a total of 11 sts; bind off 7 sts, k to end. 4 sts.
4th, 5th, 6th, 7th, and 8th rows Slip 1, k 3.
9th row With right-hand needle pick up 2 strands of last cast-on st, k first st on left-hand needle then slip strands over this st, k to end.
10th row Slip 1, k 3.
Repeat 1st–10th rows, ending with a 1st pattern row.
Bind off.

97 UNRAVELED FRINGE

Directory view, page 41

Skill level: Intermediate

 Sportweight wool

 Unraveling stitches produces an adaptable looped fringe which looks the same on both sides.

METHOD

Note: Although the yarn is doubled it has been taken from a single ball by using the end from the center of the ball along with the end from the outside.

With double yarn, cast on 9 sts.
1st row [Yo, k 2 tog, k 1] 3 times.
Repeat this row for required length.
Bind off 5 sts and fasten off.
Unravel remaining 3 sts to form fringe.
Steam any crinkles out of the fringe.

98 BEAD TASSELS

Directory view, page 41

Skill level: Easy

 Sportweight cotton

 Beads, sewing needle and strong thread, clear nail polish

 These tassels have a bead instead of a knot at the top and are attached by being knitted into the border.

METHOD

Tassels
Make one tassel for every 4 sts:
cut 4 in (10 cm) lengths of yarn—2 used for each tassel here but number will depend on size of hole in bead. Thread sewing needle with strong thread and knot ends. Into this loop fold 2 lengths of yarn (see illustration on page 12) and use needle to pull the strands through the bead. Leaving the bead almost halfway down the tassel, cut sewing thread. Make more tassels in this way.

Cast on a multiple of 4 sts plus 3.
1st row (RS) K 3, * slip loop at top of one tassel onto left-hand needle, k tog this loop and next st, k 3; repeat from * to end.
K 2 rows.
Bind off.
On each tassel in turn, place a tiny drop of nail polish near the top and slide bead over it. Leave to dry. Trim ends.

99 BOBBLES
Directory view, page 42

Skill level: Intermediate

 Sportweight wool

Bobbles are usually knitted into the fabric but they can also be suspended from the edge for a completely different effect.

METHOD

Note: To cast on 2 sts at beginning of 5th row: k in next st but do not slip it off, slip new st from right-hand needle to left-hand needle, then work the next st in the same way.

Cast on 5 sts.
1st, 2nd, 3rd, and 4th rows Slip 1, k 4.
5th row (RS) Cast on 2 sts as above, (k 1, p 1, k 1, p 1, k 1) in nearest of these sts, [turn, k 5] 5 times, turn, slip 2nd, 3rd, 4th and 5th sts one at a time over first st, working first st k 1 tbl bind off 2 sts, k 4.
6th, 7th, and 8th rows Slip 1, k 4.
Repeat 1st–8th rows.
Bind off.

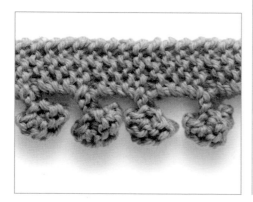

 100 KNOTTED FRINGE
Directory view, page 42

Skill level: Complex

 Sportweight wool

Knotting a multi-strand looped fringe makes a traditional-looking trim.

METHOD

Using yarn double, cast on required number of sts.
1st row (RS) * K in st but do not slip it off, bring yarn to front between needles, take it under and over left thumb to make a loop at least 2½ in (6 cm) long; having made loop at front, take yarn between needles to back, k st on left-hand needle again and slip it off; insert left-hand needle in fronts of 2 new sts on right-hand needle and k them tog tbl; repeat from * to end.
Bind off.
Cut the loops and then knot the fringe. Make each knot with a single tie around a knitting needle. Use the needle to slide the knot into position, then pull out the needle and tighten the knot.
Trim the ends.

 101 EYELETS AND TASSELS
Directory view, page 42

Skill level: Easy

 Worsted cotton
Crochet hook

There's no problem spacing tassels when they're knotted in each knitted eyelet.

METHOD

Cast on an odd number of sts.
1st row (RS) * K 2 tog, yo; repeat from * to last st, k 1.
2nd and 3rd rows K.
Bind off.
Tassels
Cut 4¾ in (12 cm) lengths of yarn—two for each eyelet. Double two strands. With wrong side facing, insert crochet hook in an eyelet and, hooking the fold of the strands, pull a loop through. Use the hook to pull the ends through the loop, enclosing the cast-on edge. Pull the ends gently to tighten the knot (see page 12 for an illustration of tassel-making). Make one tassel in each eyelet. Trim the ends.

102 CORD FRINGE
Directory view, page 42

Skill level: Complex

 Sportweight wool

Cable needle

 It takes a little practice to make cords all the same length. It's easier to wind the yarn around your own hand than to use a gauge such as a piece of card.

METHOD

Note: To make a cord: insert right-hand needle to k 1 but take yarn over spread fingers then up in front of left hand, take yarn around point of right-hand needle and k 1 in the usual way. Holding work in the left hand, insert cable needle in loop and twist in a clockwise direction 12 times (or until it won't twist any more); placing a finger in the middle of the twisted yarn, slip the loop from the cable needle onto left-hand needle, k this loop and the next st together then release the twisted yarn. If the yarn doubles itself unevenly insert cable needle at end of cord and tug gently until the twist evens out.

Cast on 4 sts.
1st row (WS) Slip 1, k 3.
2nd row Make a cord as above, k 2.
Repeat these 2 rows.
Bind off.

103 TABS
Directory view, page 43

Skill level: Intermediate

 Sportweight wool

 This unconventional fringe is made with a combination of cast-on, bind-off and turning rows, all in garter stitch.

METHOD

*Note: To cast on at beginning of 5th row: * k in st but do not slip it off, slip new st from right-hand to left-hand needle; repeat from *, working into the space between new st and previous st each time.*

Cast on 4 sts.
1st–4th rows Slip 1, k 3.
5th row (RS) Cast on 9 sts as above, k 5, turn, slip 1, k 3, turn, slip 1, k 2, turn, slip 1, k 3 (to end), turn, bind off 9 sts, k 3.
6th row Slip 1, k 3.
Repeat 1st–6th rows, ending with a 3rd pattern row.
Bind off.

104 LOOP-EDGE FRINGE
Directory view, page 43

Skill level: Easy

 Medium-weight wool

Crochet hook

 Knotting tassels on a loop-edged braid is another way to make a decorative fringe.

METHOD

Cast on 4 sts.
1st row (RS) Yo, k 2 tog, k 2.
2nd row Slip 1, k 3.
Repeat 1st and 2nd rows.
Bind off.

Tassels

Cut 4 in (10 cm) lengths of yarn—two for each tassel. Double two strands. With wrong side facing, insert crochet hook in one edge loop and, hooking the fold of the strands, pull a loop through. Use the hook to pull the ends through the tassel loop. Pull the ends gently to tighten the knot (see page 12 for an illustration of tassel-making). When all tassels are completed, trim the fringe.

105 SINGLE-LOOP FRINGE
Directory view, page 43

Skill level: Intermediate

 Worsted cotton *These loops are made on wrong-side rows and are surprisingly easy with a little practice.*

METHOD

Cast on any number of sts.
1st row (RS) K.
2nd row * Take yarn under then over 2nd finger of left hand to form a loop, k next st but do not slip it from needle, transfer st just made to the left-hand needle and k 2 tog tbl (the new st and the original st); repeat from * along the row.
3rd row * K 1 tbl; repeat from * to end.
Bind off.

106 CHAIN PICOT
Directory view, page 43

Skill level: Easy

 Worsted wool *These curious little picots are easy to make and look quite lively.*

METHOD

Cast on 4 sts.
1st row (RS) Slip 1, k 3.
2nd row As 1st row.
3rd row Make picot: k first st on left-hand needle but do not slip it off, [insert left-hand needle from left to right in new st, yarn over, complete k st] 6 times, slip st from right to left-hand needle, slip next st over it, slip st back on to right-hand needle; k remaining 3 sts.
4th row Slip 1, k 3.
Repeat 1st–4th rows, ending with a 1st pattern row.
Bind off.

107 DOUBLE TASSEL HEADS
Directory view, page 44

Skill level: Intermediate

 Worsted wool
 Wool needle *Hang small tassels from knitted loops for a richly textured effect.*

METHOD

Cast on a multiple of 6 sts plus 3.
1st and 2nd rows P.
3rd row (RS) K 3, * [k 3, turn, p 3, turn] twice, k 6; repeat from * to end.
4th and 5th rows P.
Bind off.
Make a bound tassel for each knitted loop (see page 12). These tassels consist of 8 strands of yarn, each about 4 in (10 cm) long. Trim the tassels and then, using a wool needle, take a tie through each side of a loop and knot tightly at the back. Trim the ends.

108 CUT PILE
Directory view, page 44

Skill level: Intermediate

 2 ply Jumper Weight Shetland wool

 The technique used here makes loops secure enough to be cut for a furry effect.

METHOD

Cast on 5 sts.
1st row (RS) Loop 1; k next st but do not slip it off left-hand needle, bring yarn between needles to the front, take it under and over left thumb then back between needles, k st on left-hand needle again then insert left-hand needle in front of 2 sts on right-hand needle and k these sts tog tbl; work each st along the row in this way.
2nd row K.
Repeat 1st and 2nd rows.
Bind off.
Cut the loops.

109 FOLDED LADDER LOOPS
Directory view, page 44

Skill level: Easy

 2 ply Jumper Weight Shetland wool

 These loops are simply dropped stitches, folded so that the end-of-row stitches can be joined to form a braid or used to enclose a raw edge.

METHOD

Cast on 11 sts.
1st row (RS) K 3 tbl, k 5, k 3 tbl.
2nd row P 3 tbl, p 5, p 3 tbl.
Repeat 1st and 2nd rows.
Last row Bind off 2 sts, drop next 5 sts, bind off remaining sts.
Allow dropped sts to form a ladder. Fold in half along the ladder. Either sew top edges together or enclose edge to be trimmed. If the loops are crinkled slide a knitting needle along inside the loops to tension them evenly, then steam or steam press.

110 LOOPS AND SEQUINS
Directory view, page 44

Skill level: Intermediate

 Fine mohair

Sequins and sewing needle

The light, springy yarn and dazzling sequins give this edging a particularly lively quality.

METHOD

Thread a quantity of sequins—one for each loop, a loop on each alternate row.
Cast on 4 sts.
1st row (RS) K 1, make loop: k 1 but do not slip st off left-hand needle, bring yarn between needles to the front, take it under and over your left thumb, slide a sequin along the yarn and on to this loop before taking yarn back between needles to the wrong side, k st on left-hand needle again, then slip second st on right-hand needle over this new st, k 2.
2nd row Slip 1, k 3.
Repeat 1st and 2nd rows.
Bind off.

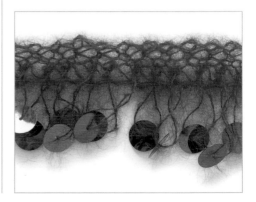

111 LOOPS AND BELLS
Directory view, page 45

Skill level: Intermediate

 Worsted cotton

 Small bells

 Make a fun fringe by knitting small bells into the loops.

METHOD

Note: Choose a strong yarn because metal bells can fray the yarn as they're being moved along.

Cast on an odd number of sts.
1st row (RS) Make a loop: k next st but do not slip it off, bring the yarn to the front between the needles, take it under then over your left thumb and back between the needles; k the st on the left-hand needle again and slip it off in the usual way, then slip the next st on the right-hand needle over it. Work each st along the row in this way.
2nd row K.
Break the yarn, thread the bells and rejoin the yarn.
3rd row * Make a loop; in next st make a loop, sliding a bell along the yarn as it is taken around the thumb; repeat from * to last st, make a loop.
Bind off.

112 POMPOM FRINGE
Directory view, page 45

Skill level: Easy

 2 ply Jumper Weight Shetland wool

Cable needle

 Few knitting skills are needed here but a little practice is necessary to make the pompoms and cords.

METHOD

Make a small pompom (see page 12), tying firmly and leaving two ends of about 3 in (8 cm) each. Knot these ends, insert a cable needle in the loop formed and twist until it won't twist any more. Take out the needle, double the cord and allow it to twist on itself. Un-knot the ends and tie them around the center of the pompom. Make the number of pompoms required.
Cast on 6 sts.
1st, 2nd, 3rd, and 4th rows Slip 1, k 5.
5th row Slip loop at end of pompom cord on to left-hand needle then k tog first st and loop, k 5.
6th row Slip 1, k 5.
Repeat 1st–6th rows, ending with a 3rd pattern row.
Bind off.

113 WILD LOOPS
Directory view, page 45

Skill level: Intermediate

 Fine mohair

 The wiry character of these loops is entirely due to the yarn—experiment with different yarns to make different effects.

METHOD

Note: Loop 1: k next st but do not slip it off, bring yarn forward between needles, take it under and over left thumb then back between needles, k st on left-hand needle again, slip second st on right-hand needle over st just made to complete loop.

Cast on 9 sts.
1st row (RS) K 1, [loop 1, k 1] 4 times.
2nd row K.
3rd row K 2, [loop 1, k 1] 3 times, k 1.
4th row K.
Repeat 1st–4th rows.
Bind off.
Catch stitch row-ends at center back to form a rouleau, taking care to leave loops free.

INSERTIONS

SEE ALSO

Knitting abbreviations, page 9
Refresher course, pages 10–13

 114 PLAIN TWO-ROW
INSERTION
Directory view, page 46

Skill level: Easy

 Worsted cotton   *This is an even simpler version of the Plain Four-row Insertion (see right).*

METHOD

Cast on 6 sts.
1st row (RS) Slip 1, skpo, yo twice, skpo, k 1.
2nd row Slip 1, k 2, p 1, k 2.
Repeat 1st and 2nd rows.
Bind off.

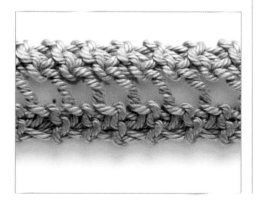

 115 PLAIN FOUR-ROW
INSERTION
Directory view, page 46

Skill level: Easy

 Worsted cotton   *For a quite different appearance these large eyelets could be threaded with ribbon.*

METHOD

Cast on 6 sts.
1st row (RS) Slip 1, k 5.
2nd row As 1st row.
3rd row Slip 1, skpo, yo twice, skpo, k 1.
4th row Slip 1, k 2, p 1, k 2.
Repeat 1st–4th rows, ending with a
1st pattern row.
Bind off.

CROSS STITCH
Directory view, page 46

Skill level: Complex

 Sportweight wool   This is an example of a fancy stitch making a beautiful horizontal panel.

METHOD

Cast on a multiple of 8 sts.
1st row (RS) K.
2nd row K.
3rd row * Insert needle in next st and wrap yarn 4 times around needle, complete the k st leaving all wraps on needle; repeat from * to end.
4th row * With yarn at back slip 8 sts, dropping extra wraps to form long sts, insert left-hand needle into the first 4 of these sts and pass them over the second 4, return all sts to the left-hand needle and k all sts in this order; repeat from * to end.
5th row K.
Bind off.

SINGLE FAGGOT STITCH
Directory view, page 46

Skill level: Easy

 Worsted cotton   This variation of faggot stitch creates a very open zigzag mesh and a firm border.

METHOD

Cast on 6 sts.
1st row (RS) Slip 1, k 2, yo, k 2 tog, k 1.
2nd row Slip 1, p 2, yo, p 2 tog tbl, k 1.
Repeat 1st and 2nd rows.
Bind off.

COIN EYELET
Directory view, page 47

Skill level: Intermediate

 Sportweight unbrushed mohair   This large eyelet is made with an unusual combination of single and double decreases.

METHOD

Note: dec2r—decrease 2 sts to the right: k 2 tog, slip the new st onto the left-hand needle, slip the next st over it then slip it back onto the right-hand needle; sk2po—decrease 2 sts to the left: slip one st, k 2 tog, pass slipped st over.

Cast on 14 sts.
1st row (WS) K 2, p 10, k 2.
2nd row K 2, yo, skpo, dec2r, sk2po, k 2 tog, yo, k 2. 10 sts.
3rd row K 2, p 3, lift strand in front of next st on to left-hand needle and work (k 1, p 1, k 1, p 1) into it, p 3, k 2. 14 sts.
4th row K 2, yo, skpo, k 6, k 2 tog, yo, k 2.
Repeat 1st–4th rows.
Bind off.

119 COCKLESHELL

Directory view, page 47

Skill level: Intermediate

 Sportweight wool   *This is simply a single pattern repeat of an old Shetland lace stitch.*

METHOD

Cast on 15 sts.
1st row (RS) K 2 tog, yo, k 1, k 2 tog, k 5, skpo, k 1, yo, skpo. 13 sts.
2nd row P 2, k 9, p 2.
3rd row K 2 tog, yo, k 3, [yo, k 1] 3 times, yo, k 3, yo, skpo. 17 sts.
4th row P 2, k 2, p 9, k 2, p 2.
5th row K 2 tog, yo, k 1, k 2 tog, k 7, skpo, k 1, yo, skpo. 15 sts.
6th row P 2, k 2, p 7, k 2, p 2.
Repeat 1st–6th rows.
Bind off.

120 MOCK CABLE

Directory view, page 47

Skill level: Intermediate

 Sportweight wool   *This uses the same technique as Cross stitch (see page 100) but the rows run in the opposite direction.*

METHOD

Cast on 14 sts.
1st row (RS) Slip 1, k 13.
2nd, 4th, and 6th rows Slip 1, k 2, p 8, k 3.
3rd and 5th rows As 1st row.
7th row Slip 1, k 2, [insert needle in next st and wrap yarn 4 times around needle, complete the k st leaving all wraps on the needle] 8 times, k 3.
8th row Slip 1, k 2, with yarn at front sl 8 sts, dropping extra wraps to form long sts, insert left-hand needle into the first 4 of these sts and pass them over the second 4, return all sts to the left-hand needle and p all 8 sts in this order, k 3.
9th and 11th rows As 1st row.
10th and 12th rows As 2nd row.
Repeat 1st–12th rows.
Bind off.

121 DIAGONAL STRIPE

Directory view, page 47

Skill level: Intermediate

 Sportweight wool   *Lacy diagonals are offset by neat faggot stitch edgings.*

METHOD

Cast on 12 sts.
1st row (RS) Slip 1, yo, p 2 tog, k 1, yo, k 2 tog, k 3, yo, p 2 tog, k 1.
2nd row Slip 1, yo, p 2 tog, p 6, yo, p 2 tog, k 1.
3rd row Slip 1, yo, p 2 tog, k 2, yo, k 2 tog, k 2, yo, p 2 tog, k 1.
4th row As 2nd row.
5th row Slip 1, yo, p 2 tog, k 3, yo, k 2 tog, k 1, yo, p 2 tog, k 1.
6th row As 2nd row.
7th row Slip 1, yo, p 2 tog, k 4, yo, k 2 tog, yo, p 2 tog, k 1.
8th row As 2nd row.
Repeat 1st–8th rows.
Bind off.

122 DAISY

Directory view, page 48

Skill level: Intermediate

 Sportweight cotton

 Child's drawing-book daisies are made with simple double increases and paired decreases.

METHOD

Cast on 12 sts.
1st and 3rd rows (RS) Slip 1, k 11.
2nd and 4th rows Slip 1, k 1, p 8, k 2.
5th row Slip 1, k 3, k 2 tog, yo twice, skpo, k 4.
6th row Slip 1, k 1, p 3, k 1, p 4, k 2.
7th row Slip 1, k 1, [k 2 tog, yo twice, skpo] twice, k 2.
8th row Slip 1, k 1, p 1, k 1, p 3, k 1, p 2, k 2.
9th row As 5th row.
10th row As 6th row.
11th row As 7th row.
12th row As 8th row.
13th row As 5th row.
14th row As 6th row.
Repeat 1st–14th rows, ending with a 3rd pattern row.
Bind off.

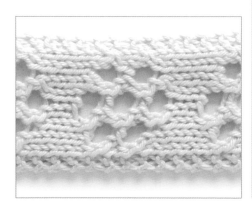

123 GARTER-STITCH DIAMONDS

Directory view, page 48

Skill level: Intermediate

 Sportweight cotton

 Large eyelets in plain garter stitch have an old-fashioned simplicity.

METHOD

Cast on 16 sts.
1st row (RS) Sl 1, k 15.
2nd row As 1st row.
3rd row Slip 1, k 5, k 2 tog, yo twice, skpo, k 6.
4th row Slip 1, k 6, (k 1, p 1) in double yo, k 7.
5th row Slip 1, k 3, [k 2 tog, yo twice, skpo] twice, k 4.
6th row Slip 1, k to end, working (k 1, p 1) in each double yo.
7th row Slip 1, k 1, [k 2 tog, yo twice, skpo] 3 times, k 2.
8th row As 6th row.
9th row As 5th row.
10th row As 6th row.
11th row As 3rd row.
12th row As 4th row.
Repeat 1st–12th rows, ending with a 1st pattern row.
Bind off.

124 DAISY CHAIN

Directory view, page 48

Skill level: Intermediate

 Sportweight cotton

Neat little daisies are strung out on a garter stitch background.

METHOD

Cast on 10 sts.
1st row (RS) Slip 1, k 9.
2nd, 3rd, and 4th rows As 1st row.
5th row Slip 1, k 2, k 2 tog, yo twice, k 2 tog, k 3.
6th row Slip 1, k 3, p 1, k 5.
7th row Slip 1, k 1, k 2 tog, [yo twice, k 2 tog] twice, k 2. 11 sts.
8th row Slip 1, k 3, p 1, k 1, p 1, k 4.
9th row Slip 1, k 1, k 2 tog, k 1, yo twice, k 2 tog, k 2 tog tbl, k 2. 10 sts.
10th row Slip 1, k 4, p 1, k 4.
Repeat 1st–10th rows, ending with a 3rd pattern row.
Bind off.

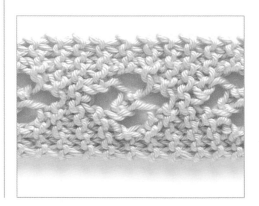

125 HONEY BEE

Directory view, page 48

Skill level: Complex

 Worsted cotton

 A dainty open stitch can look surprisingly attractive in a substantial yarn.

METHOD

Note: To cast on 4 sts on 5th row: [lift yarn with left index finger, take right-hand needle from back to front under strand behind finger, pull yarn to tighten loop on needle] 4 times.

Cast on 16 sts.
1st row (RS) Slip 1, p 1, k 4, k 2 tog, yo, skpo, k 4, p 1, k 1. 15 sts.
2nd row Slip 1, k 1, p 3, p 2 tog tbl, drop previous yo off needle, yo twice, p 2 tog, p 3, k 2. 14 sts.
3rd row Slip 1, p 1, k 2, k 2 tog, drop previous yarn-overs, yo 3 times, skpo, k 2, p 1, k 1. 13 sts.

4th row Slip 1, k 1, p 1, p 2 tog tbl, drop previous yarn-overs, yo 4 times, p 2 tog, p 1, k 2. 12 sts.
5th row Slip 1, p 1, k 2 tog, drop previous yarn-overs, cast on 4 sts on right-hand needle as above, k 1 under 4 loose strands of dropped yarn-overs, yo, k 1 again under 4 loose strands, cast on 4 sts on right-hand needle as above, skpo, p 1, k 1. 17 sts.
6th row Slip 1, k 1, p 5, p 2 tog, p 6, k 2. 16 sts.
Repeat 1st–6th rows.
Bind off.

126 SKELETON LEAF

Directory view, page 49

Skill level: Intermediate

 Sportweight cotton

 Because the stitch count remains the same on every row this leaf is clearly defined but quite flat.

METHOD

Note: sk2po—slip one st knitwise, k 2 tog, pass slipped st over.

Cast on 17 sts.
1st row (RS) Slip 1, k 3, [k 2 tog, yo] twice, k 1, [yo, skpo] twice, k 4.
2nd row Slip 1, k 5, p 5, k 6.
3rd row Slip 1, k 2, k 2 tog, yo, k 2 tog, k 1, [yo, k 1] twice, skpo, yo, skpo, k 3.
4th row Slip 1, k 4, p 7, k 5.
5th row Slip 1, k 1, k 2 tog, yo, k 2 tog, k 2, yo, k 1, yo, k 2, skpo, yo, skpo, k 2.
6th row Slip 1, k 3, p 9, k 4.
7th row Slip 1, k 2 tog, yo, k 2 tog, k 3, yo, k 1, yo, k 3, skpo, yo, skpo, k 1.
8th row Slip 1, k 2, p 11, k 3.

9th row Slip 1, k 2, yo, skpo, k 7, k 2 tog, yo, k 3.
10th row Slip 1, k 3, p 9, k 4.
11th row Slip 1, k 3, yo, skpo, k 5, k 2 tog, yo, k 4.
12th row Slip 1, k 4, p 7, k 5.
13th row Slip 1, k 4, yo, skpo, k 3, k 2 tog, yo, k 5.
14th row Slip 1, k 5, p 5, k 6.
15th row Slip 1, k 5, yo, skpo, k 1, k 2 tog, yo, k 6.
16th row Slip 1, k 6, p 3, k 7.
17th row Slip 1, k 6, yo, sk2po, yo, k 7.
18th row Slip 1, k 7, p 1, k 8.
Repeat 1st–18th rows.
Bind off.

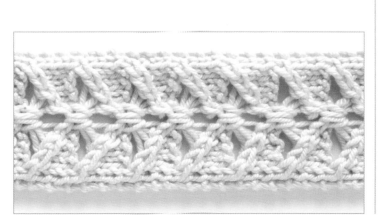

127 LACY ZIGZAG
Directory view, page 49

Skill level: Intermediate

 Sportweight cotton

 Knotted edges and the sloping decreases of the zigzag lace are the main ingredients of this classic insertion.

METHOD

Cast on 14 sts.
1st row (WS) K 2, p 10, k 2.
2nd row K 2 tog, yo, k 4, [k 2 tog, yo] twice, k 2, yo, k 2 tog.
3rd, 5th, 7th, 9th, and 11th rows As 1st row.
4th row K 2 tog, yo, k 3, [k 2 tog, yo] twice, k 3, yo, k 2 tog.
6th row K 2 tog, yo, k 2, [k 2 tog, yo] twice, k 4, yo, k 2 tog.
8th row K 2 tog, yo, k 2, [yo, skpo] twice, k 4, yo, k 2 tog.
10th row K 2 tog, yo, k 3, [yo, skpo] twice, k 3, yo, k 2 tog.
12th row K 2 tog, yo, k 4, [yo, skpo] twice, k 2, yo, k 2 tog.
Repeat 1st–12th rows, ending with a 2nd pattern row.
Bind off.

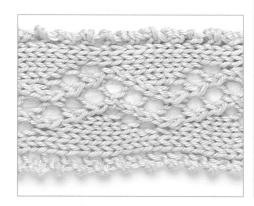

128 TRADITIONAL
Directory view, page 49

Skill level: Easy

 Worsted cotton

 A double line of faggot stitch is the main ingredient of this open insertion.

METHOD

Note: sk2po—slip one st knitwise, k 2 tog, pass slipped st over.

Cast on 9 sts.
1st row (RS) Slip 1, k 2 tog, yo, sk2po, yo, skpo, k 1. 7 sts.
2nd row Slip 1, k 1, yo, k 3, yo, k 2. 9 sts.
Repeat 1st and 2nd rows.
Bind off.

129 CHECKERS
Directory view, page 49

Skill level: Intermediate

 Sportweight cotton

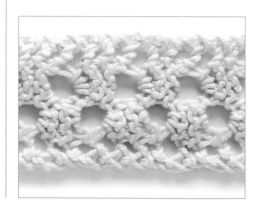 *This is not quite as simple as it looks, but the result is a bold, open design.*

METHOD

Note: The stitch pattern is made up of two 3-row repeats, so rows 4, 5, and 6 are the same as rows 1, 2, and 3 but on the opposite side of the work.

Cast on 12 sts.
1st row Yo, p 2 tog, k 4, yo, slip 4 sts one at a time from right-hand needle over the yo, k 4, yo, p 2 tog. 9 sts.
2nd row Yo, p 2 tog, k 4, yo, k 1, yo, p 2 tog. 10 sts.
3rd row Yo, p 2 tog, k 1, (k 1, p 1, k 1) in yo of previous row, k 4, yo, p 2 tog. 12 sts.
4th row As 1st row.
5th row As 2nd row.
6th row As 3rd row.
Repeat 1st–6th rows, ending with a 3rd or 6th pattern row.
Bind off.

ADDITIONS

SEE ALSO

Knitting abbreviations, page 9
Refresher course, pages 10–13

130 BELL

Directory view, page 50

Skill level: Intermediate

 Worsted wool in turquoise (A) and pink (B)
2 double-pointed needles

 Made from the top downward and finished with a picot bind-off, this bell toggle has a cord which can be knitted to any length.

METHOD

With A, cast on 3 sts.
1st row (RS) (K 1, p 1, k 1) in each st. 9 sts.
2nd row P.
3rd row [K 1, m 1] 8 times, k 1. 17 sts.
Beg with a p row, work 7 rows st–st.
11th row * Cast on 2, bind off 4, slip st from right-hand needle to left-hand needle; repeat from * to end. Fasten off.

Cord

With RS facing and using double-pointed needles, pick up and k one st in each loop made by increasing on first row. 3 sts.
Do not turn work.
1st row (RS) Slide sts to end of needle, taking yarn behind and across sts, k 3.
Without turning, repeat this row until cord is required length. Bind off.

Making up

Join the seam of the bell.
With B, make a small pompom (see page 12) and sew it inside the bell.

131 ROSE LEAF

Directory view, page 50

Skill level: Easy

 Sportweight wool
2 double-pointed needles

 These simple stockinette stitch leaves can be made in a single shade of green or in varying colors.

METHOD

Note: s2kpo—sl 2 sts as if to k 2 tog, k 1, pass slipped sts over.

Leaf (make 3)
Cast on 2 sts.
1st row (RS) Kfb, k 1. 3 sts.
2nd and WS rows P.
3rd row K 1, [m 1, k 1] twice. 5 sts.
5th row K 2, m 1, k 1, m 1, k 2. 7 sts.
7th row K 3, m 1, k 1, m 1, k 3. 9 sts.
Beginning with a p row, work 3 rows straight.
11th row Skpo, k 5, k 2 tog. 7 sts.
13th row Skpo, k 3, k 2 tog. 5 sts.
15th row Skpo, k 1, k 2 tog. 3 sts.
17th row S2kpo.
Fasten off remaining stitch.

Stem

Make a 2 in (5 cm) long cord (see page 13).
Bind off, working k 1, k 2 tog. Press. Starting with center leaf, sew leaves to bound-off end of stem.

132 ROSE

Directory view, page 50

Skill level: Intermediate

 Worsted wool

 The rose petals are made in a continuous piece and then coiled, the shaped edge curling naturally.

METHOD

Note: kfb—knit in front then back of st; pfb—purl in front then back of st.

Cast on 5 sts.
Small petals
1st row Kfb, k 4. 6 sts.
2nd row P 4, pfb, p 1. 7 sts.
3rd row K 7.
4th row P 7.
5th row K 1, k 2 tog, k 4. 6 sts.
6th row P 3, p 2 tog, p 1. 5 sts.
Repeat 1st–6th rows 3 times more. Do not break yarn.

Medium petals
1st and 3rd rows Kfb, k to end.
2nd and 4th rows P to last 2 sts, pfb, p 1.
5th and 7th rows K 9.
6th and 8th rows P 9.
9th and 11th rows K 1, k 2 tog, k to end.
10th and 12th rows P to last 3 sts, p 2 tog, p 1. 5 sts.
Repeat 1st–12th rows twice more. Do not break yarn.

Large petals
1st, 3rd, and 5th rows Kfb, k to end.
2nd, 4th, and 6th rows P to last 2 sts, pfb, p 1.
7th, 9th, and 11th rows K 11.
8th, 10th, and 12th rows P 11.

13th, 15th, and 17th rows K 1, k 2 tog, k to end.
14th, 16th, and 18th rows P to last 3 sts, p 2 tog, p 1. 5 sts.
Repeat 1st–18th rows twice more.
Next row K 1, k 2 tog, k 2.
Next row P 1, p 2 tog, p 1.
Next row K 1, k 2 tog.
Next row P 2 tog.
Fasten off.

Making up

Press. With reverse stockinette st to outside, roll up loosely from the cast-on end. Lightly stitch straight edges together to form a flat base then push up center. Gather and stitch outside edge at base. Turn back petals and steam if necessary.

133 ROSEBUD

Directory view, page 50

Skill level: Intermediate

 Worsted wool in red (A) and green (B)

2 double-pointed needles

 Like the rose (see left), the rosebud is a single piece of stocking stitch with a shaped edge which curls to form petals.

METHOD

Petals
With A, cast on 4 sts.
1st and 3rd rows Kfb, k to end.
2nd and 4th rows P to last 2 sts, pfb, p 1.
Beg with a k row, work 4 rows stockinette st.
9th row K 1, k 2 tog, k to end.
10th row P to last 3 sts, p 2 tog, p 1. 6 sts.
Repeat 1st–10th rows once more. 8 sts. Repeat 1st–10th rows once more. 10 sts. Bind off.

Base
With B, cast on 4 sts.
1st row (RS) P.
2nd row Cast on 3 by knitting on (see page 10), bind off 3 sts, k 3. 4 sts.
3rd row P.
4th row K.

Repeat 1st–4th rows 4 times more.
Bind off.
With RS facing, pick up and k 12 sts along straight edge. P 1 row.
Next row [K 2 tog] 6 times. 6 sts. P 1 row.
Next row [K 2 tog] 3 times. 3 sts. Do not break yarn. Slip sts onto double-pointed needle and work 1 in (2.5 cm) cord (see page 13).
Bind off.

Making up

Press petals and coil them from the long end with reverse stockinette st to the outside. Gather along straight edge and sew. Join the seam of the base and sew the bud inside it.

134 BRAID LEAF

Directory view, page 50

Skill level: Easy

 2 ply
Jumper Weight
Shetland wool

2 double-pointed needles,
thread, and needle

 This leaf is based
on military-style
frogging.

METHOD

With double-pointed needles, cast on 3 sts by the thumb method (see page 10).
* Without turning, slide the sts to the opposite end of the needle, take the yarn firmly from the left across the wrong side of the sts and k 3; transfer needle to the left hand and repeat from * until you have a cord approximately 16 in (41 cm) long.
Bind off, working k 1, k 2 tog.

Making up On a flat surface, starting from the halfway point, make a central loop in the cord then curve the cord to make 3 more loops along one side, using sewing thread to baste in position. Baste the opposite side to match. On the wrong side, catch stitch adjoining loops and the 2 tail ends which form the stem. Press lightly.

135 LOOP FLOWER

Directory view, page 51

Skill level: Intermediate

 Worsted wool
in mauve (A)
and pink (B)

 A shaped strip of
loop-stitch knitting
joined into a ring
makes a simple
mop-head flower.

METHOD

Note: Loop 1— k next st but do not slip it off left-hand needle, bring yarn forward between needles, take it under and over left thumb then back between needles, k st on left-hand needle again, slip second st on right-hand needle over st just made.

With A, cast on 19 sts.
1st row (RS) Loop 1 in every st.
2nd row K 1, [k 2 tog, k 1] 6 times. 13 sts.
Change to B.
3rd row As 1st row.
4th row K 1, [k 2 tog, k 1] 4 times. 9 sts.
5th row As 1st row.
Bind off, working [k 2 tog] 4 times, k 1.

Making up
Coil into a ring on wrong side.

136 FERN LEAF

Directory view, page 51

Skill level: Intermediate

 Worsted wool

 This naturally curving
stem and leaves are
made with the cast-on
and bind-off method of
creating picots.

METHOD

*Note: After the initial cast-on, use this method to cast on: * k in next st but do not drop st off left-hand needle, transfer new st to left-hand needle; repeat from *, working into new st each time.*

Cast on 19 sts.
Bind off 6 sts, [transfer st from right-hand needle to left-hand needle, cast on 4 sts, bind off 6 sts] twice, [transfer st from right-hand to left-hand needle, cast on 3 sts, bind off 5 sts] twice, [transfer st from right-hand to left-hand needle, cast on 2 sts, bind off 3 sts] twice, transfer st from right-hand to left-hand needle, cast on one st, bind off 3 sts.
Fasten off.

137 CORNFLOWER

Directory view, page 51

Skill level: Easy

 Worsted wool in deep blue (A) and pale blue (B)

 This is simply a length of picots coiled up into a flowerhead, and could easily be made larger or smaller.

METHOD

*Note: On 3rd row cast on: * k next st but do not drop it off left-hand needle, transfer new st from right-hand to left-hand needle; repeat from *, working into new st each time.*

With A, cast on 4 sts.
1st row (RS) K.
2nd row P.
3rd row Cast on 4 sts as above, bind off 4 sts, k 3. 4 sts.
4th row P.
Repeat 3rd and 4th rows 9 times more.
Change to B.
Repeat 3rd and 4th rows 24 times more.
Bind off.

Making up
Coil up with knit side to inside.
Sew all layers around coil.

138 BOBBLE

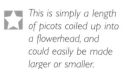

Directory view, page 51

Skill level: Easy

 Sportweight wool Absorbent cotton

 Soft and round, this little ball can be made larger simply by using a thicker yarn.

METHOD

Cast on 5 sts.
1st row (RS) Kfb 4 times, k 1. 9 sts.
2nd and WS rows P.
3rd row K 1, [m 1, k 1] 8 times. 17 sts.
5th row K 1, [m 1, k 2] 8 times. 25 sts.
Beg with a p row, work 5 rows stockinette st.
11th row K 1, [k 2 tog, k 1] 8 times. 17 sts.
13th row K 1, k 2 tog 8 times. 9 sts.
15th row K 1, k 2 tog 4 times. 5 sts.
Fasten off by taking yarn through these 5 sts.

Making up
Join the seam, taking in half a st from each edge and stuffing the ball with absorbent cotton before completing. Lightly press seam and shapings. Make a 2 in (5 cm) chain (see page 13) and attach to the top as a loop.

139 BLUE DAISY

Directory view, page 51

Skill level: Intermediate

 Worsted yarn in blue (A) and yellow (B)

The main part of this flower is knitted in one piece, shaped with turning rows.

METHOD

With A, cast on 6 sts.
1st row (WS) K.
2nd row (K 1, p 1, k 1, p 1, k 1) in first st, turn, k 5, turn, p 5, turn, k 5, turn, p 2 tog twice, p 1, take yarn to back and on right-hand needle slip 2nd and 3rd sts over first to complete petal, * p 3, turn, slip 1, k 3.
3rd row P.
Repeat 1st–3rd rows 6 times more, then work 1st and 2nd rows to *.
Bind off purlwise.

Making up
Gather center by running a thread through the sts of the short edge. Join cast-on and bound-off edges. Press center but not petals. With B, make a pompom (see page 12) to fill center and sew in place.

STAR

Directory view, page 52

Skill level: Easy

 Sportweight cotton

 Simple diamond-shaped sections make a five-point star.

METHOD

Note: s2kpo—sl 2 sts as if to k 2 tog, k 1, pass slipped sts over.

Put a slip knot on the needle.
1st row (RS) (K 1, p 1, k 1) in st. 3 sts.
2nd and WS rows P.
3rd row K 1, [m 1, k 1] twice. 5 sts.
5th row K 1, m 1, k 3, m 1, k 1. 7 sts.
7th row K 1, m 1, k 5, m 1, k 1. 9 sts.
9th row K 1, k 2 tog, k 3, skpo, k 1. 7 sts.
11th row K 1, k 2 tog, k 1, skpo, k 1. 5 sts.
13th row K 1, s2kpo, k 1. 3 sts.
15th row S2kpo. 1 st. Fasten off.
Make 4 more diamonds.

Making up
Placing slip knots to the center and taking in one st from each edge, join the five sections from 1st–8th rows. Press.

 MARGUERITE

Directory view, page 52

Skill level: Easy

 Worsted cotton (A) and multistrand yarn (B)

 Simple casting on and binding off produces petals that can be made to any length, although they will curl if made very long.

METHOD

Note: 2nd row cast-on: k in next st but do not drop it off left-hand needle, transfer new st from right hand to left-hand needle, * k between sts to make next st, transfer new st from right-hand needle to left-hand needle; repeat from * 4 times.

With A, cast on 3 sts.
1st row K.
2nd row Cast on 6 sts as above, bind off 6 sts, k 2. 3 sts.
Repeat 1st and 2nd rows 13 times more, binding off all 9 sts on last row.

Making up
Run the last end through the edge sts to gather them in the center then join 3 cast-on sts to last 3 bound-off sts to make a ring. Press. With B, make a pompom (see page 12) and attach it in the center.

 HEART

Directory view, page 52

Skill level: Intermediate

 Worsted cotton

 Symmetrical shaping makes a heart that's almost as precise as a paper cutout.

METHOD

Cast on 2 sts.
1st row (RS) Kfb, k 1. 3 sts.
2nd and WS rows P.
3rd row K 1, [m 1, k 1] twice. 5 sts.
5th row K 2, m 1, k 1, m 1, k 2. 7 sts.
7th row K 3, m 1, k 1, m 1, k 3. 9 sts.
9th row K 4, m 1, k 1, m 1, k 4. 11 sts.
11th row K 5, m 1, k 1, m 1, k 5. 13 sts.
13th row K 6, increase by working k in back loop of st below next then k in next st as usual, k 6. 14 sts.
15th row Skpo, k 3, k 2 tog, turn.
Continue on these 5 sts only and leave remaining sts on a st holder.
17th row Skpo, k 1, k 2 tog. 3 sts.
18th row P 3 tog tbl. Fasten off.
Next row (RS) Rejoin yarn to inner end of remaining sts, skpo, k 3, k 2 tog. 5 sts.
Next RS row Skpo, k 1, k 2 tog. 3 sts.
Next row P 3 tog. Fasten off.

143 BUTTERFLY

Directory view, page 52

Skill level: Complex

 Sportweight cotton in turquoise (A), lime (B), and charcoal (C) 2 double-pointed needles

 The butterfly's construction is simple—the wings are doubled for stability and the body is a cord, with a bobble for the head.

METHOD

First wing
With A, cast on 4 sts.
1st row K.
* **2nd, 4th, 6th, and 8th rows** P.
3rd row K 1, m 1, k 2, m 1, k 1. 6 sts.
5th, 7th, and 9th rows K 1, m 1, k to last st, m 1, k 1.
10th row P 12.
11th, 12th, and 13th rows K.
14th row P.
Continue with A, except for sts indicated B.
15th row Skpo, k 3, k 2 B, k 3, k 2 tog. 10 sts.
16th row P 3, p 4 B, p 3.
17th row Skpo, k 1, k 4 B, k 1, k 2 tog. 8 sts.
18th row P 2, p 4 B, p 2.
19th row Skpo, k 1, k 2 B, k 1, k 2 tog. 6 sts.
Break off B and continue with A.
20th row P.
21st row Skpo, k 2, k 2 tog. 4 sts.
22nd row P.
Bind off.

Second wing
With RS facing and using A, pick up and k 4 sts along cast-on edge of first wing. Complete as first wing from *.

Body
With double-pointed needles and C, make a 1¼ in (3 cm) long cord (see page 13), working last row slip 1, k 2 tog, pass slipped st over.
Next row (RS) (K 1, p 1, k 1, p 1, k 1) in rem st. 5 sts. Turn.
Next row K.
Next row Slip 2nd, 3rd, 4th, and 5th sts over first st, then k this st tbl.
Fasten off, leaving an end for an antenna.

Making up
Make a second single-strand antenna. Press wings, fold along k ridge and join edges with running stitch in edge sts on the right side. Sew on body.

144 TUCKED FLOWER

Directory view, page 52

Skill level: Complex

 Worsted cotton in yellow (A) and cream (B)

 With tucked loops for petals this is a sturdy, stylized flower.

METHOD

With A, cast on 9 sts.
1st row (RS) Kfb in each st. 18 sts.
2nd row K.
Break off A and join B.

First petal
1st row (RS) K 3, turn.
Leaving remaining sts on spare yarn, continue on these sts only:
* p 3, k 3; repeat from * 5 times more then p 3 again.
Next row (RS) Join petal into a loop: [insert right-hand needle in next st, then in back loop of corresponding st of last row of A and k 2 tog] 3 times.
Do not break yarn.

On remaining sts work 5 more petals as first petal.
Bind off all 18 sts.

Making up
Gather into a ring by running first end through sts of cast-on row. Join edges to complete the ring.

145 SUNFLOWER
Directory view, page 52

Skill level: Complex

 Sportweight cotton in olive (A) and lime (B)

 Double increases and decreases shape the seed stitch center of the sunflower, while the petals are three-stitch picots.

METHOD

Note: kpk—(k in front, p in front, k in back) of st; pkp—(p in front, k in back, p in front) of st; cast-on for petals: k next st but do not slip off left-hand needle, transfer new st from right-hand needle to left-hand needle, k in previous new st to cast on next st.

Center
With A, cast on 5 sts.
1st row (RS) Kpk, p 1, k 1, pkp, k 1. 9 sts.
2nd, 3rd, and 4th rows K 1, * p 1, k 1; repeat from * to end.
5th row Kpk, [p 1, k 1] 3 times, pkp, k 1. 13 sts.
6th–14th rows As 2nd row.
15th row K 1, p 3 tog, [k 1, p 1] twice, k 1, p 3 tog, k 1. 9 sts.
16th, 17th, and 18th rows As 2nd row.

Bind off, working k 1, p 3 tog, k 1, p 3 tog, k 1 across row.

Petals
With RS facing and using B, pick up and k one st from edge, transfer this st to left-hand needle, cast on 3 sts as above, bind off 3 sts, * pick up one st from edge, slip st already on right-hand needle over it then transfer new st to left-hand needle, cast on 3 sts, bind off 3 sts; repeat from * around edge. Fasten off.
Press lightly.

146 BLUEBELLS
Directory view, page 53

Skill level: Intermediate

 Sportweight wool in blue (A) and green (B)
2 double-pointed needles

 Each of these little bluebells has a picot hem for petals and a knitted cord for a stem.

METHOD

Note: s2kpo—sl 2 sts as if to k 2 tog, k 1, pass slipped sts over.

Flower
With A, cast on 15 sts.
1st row K.
2nd row P.
3rd row [K 2 tog, yo] 7 times, k 1.
Beginning with a p row, work 3 rows stockinette st.
7th row (RS) Join hem: [insert right-hand needle in next st, then in back loop of corresponding st of cast-on row and k 2 tog] 15 times.
Beginning with a p row, work 5 rows stockinette st.

13th row S2kpo 5 times. 5 sts.
P 1 row.
Break yarn and run end through sts to gather them.

Stem
With double-pointed needles and B, make a 2¼ in (6 cm) long cord (see page 13).

Making up
Join seam of flower. Attach stem. With B, make a small tassel (see page 12) and attach inside flower.

147 SNOWDROPS
Directory view, page 53

Skill level: Easy

 Sportweight wool in white (A) and pale green (B)

 The petals of this flower exploit the natural tendency of stocking stitch to curl at the edges.

METHOD

Petal
With A, cast on 4 sts.
1st row (RS) Slip 1, k 3.
2nd row Slip 1, p 3.
3rd row Slip 1, m 1, k 2, m 1, k 1. 6 sts.
4th row P.
5th row Slip 1, m 1, k 4, m 1, k 1. 8 sts.
Beg with a p row, work 5 rows stockinette st.
11th row [K 2 tog] 4 times. 4 sts.
12th row P.
Break yarn and leave sts on a spare needle.
Make 2 more petals.

Base
Next row (RS) With A, k 4 sts of each petal. 12 sts.
Beg with a p row, work 3 rows stockinette st, then change to B and work 4 rows stockinette st. Bind off, working k 2 tog along row.

Stem
With B, cast on 18 sts.
Bind off.

Making up
Do not press. Join side seam of base. Insert stem in opening and secure.

---

 148 KNITTED TASSEL
Directory view, page 53

Skill level: Intermediate

 *Sportweight wool
Absorbent cotton*

A tassel that's knitted (not fringed) is a quirky item but it gives many possibilities for decoration.

METHOD

Note: s2kpo—slip 2 sts as if to k 2 tog, k 1, pass slipped sts over.

Cast on 33 sts.
1st row (RS) P.
2nd row P.
3rd row K 1, [k 2 tog, k 1, yo, k 1, yo, k 1, skpo, k 1] 4 times.
4th and WS rows P.
Repeat 3rd and 4th rows 3 times.
11th row K 1, [k 2 tog, k 3, skpo, k 1] 4 times. 25 sts.
13th row K 1, [k 2 tog, k 1, skpo, k 1] 4 times. 17 sts.
15th row K 1, [s2kpo, k 1] 4 times. 9 sts.
Beginning with a p row, work 3 rows stockinette st.
19th row K 1, kfb 8 times. 17 sts.

Beg with a p row, work 5 rows stockinette st.
25th row K 1, [k 2 tog] 8 times. 9 sts.
26th row (WS) P 1, [p 2 tog] 4 times. 5 sts.
To fasten off, take yarn through remaining sts.

Making up
Press straight part of tassel. Join seam, taking in ½ st from each edge. Fill head of tassel with absorbent cotton and complete seam. Bind below the head of tassel (see page 12). Make a chain 2 in (5 cm) long (see page 13), fold into a loop and attach to head of tassel.

149 CORD PULL

Directory view, page 53

Skill level: Intermediate

 Sportweight cotton

 Beads, needle and strong thread, metal or plastic ring, 2 double-pointed needles

 This is a simple piece of rib with beads worked into the cast-on row and the rib folded around a ring. The knitted cord can be made to any length.

METHOD

Thread beads, one for every knit st of the rib (see page 13). The ring shown is 1 in (2.5 cm) in diameter and requires 21 sts. Cast on an odd number of sts: using the end of yarn before the threaded beads, put a slip knot on the needle, * slide a bead along the yarn and up to the needle, pushing the bead through as the st is made, cast on one st by the thumb method (see page 10), cast on one st without a bead; repeat from *.
1st row (RS) P 1, * k 1, p 1; repeat from * to end.

2nd row K 1, * p 1, k 1; repeat from * to end.
Repeat these 2 rows twice more.
Bind off loosely.
Make a cord 1½ in (4 cm) long (see page 13).

Making up

Attach cord to ring. Fold rib around ring.
Join ends of rib, enclosing cord.
On wrong side, catch down bound-off edge.

150 CHRISTMAS STOCKING

Directory view, page 53

Skill level: Easy

 2 ply Jumper Weight Shetland wool

 This is not quite conventional as it's made in one piece with a seam along the side and foot, but the result looks like a tiny traditional stocking.

METHOD

Cast on 15 sts.
1st row (RS) K 1, [p 1, k 1] 7 times.
2nd row P 1, [k 1, p 1] 7 times.
Repeat these 2 rows once.
Beginning with a k row, work 10 rows stockinette st.

Shaping

1st row (RS) K 6, m 1, [k 1, m 1] 3 times, k 6. 19 sts.
2nd, 4th, and 6th rows P.
3rd row K 8, m 1, [k 1, m 1] 3 times, k 8. 23 sts.
5th row K 2, k 2 tog, k 15, skpo, k 2. 21 sts.
7th row K 2, k 2 tog, k 4, skpo, k 1, k 2 tog, k 4, skpo, k 2. 17 sts.
Bind off purlwise.

Making up

Taking in half a st from each edge on rib, join back and foot seam. Press. Make a 2 in (5 cm) chain (see page 13), loop it and attach to top of seam.

PROJECTS

The projects in this chapter are designed to provide ideas and inspiration for using the trims in the directory. As well as looking at how the trims can be applied to existing garments and soft furnishings the projects also demonstrate how varying the yarns used in the directory can bring a whole new look to the trims.

PROJECT 1: BABY OVERALLS

These plain overalls have been dressed up for special-occasion wear.

Lengths of Bell Ruffle (page 80) in sportweight yarn have been knitted to fit around the yoke and ankles. You will need to experiment with a small section of ruffle in order to calculate the number of pattern repeats for the length required. Using matching sewing thread to backstitch along the furrow beneath the bind-off row at the top holds the ruffle in place invisibly. The neck of a baby's sweater could also be trimmed in this way to look like a little pierrot collar, as long as there is an opening and fastening.

PROJECT 2: HERB CUSHION

Pretty and sweet-smelling, a herb cushion makes an attractive gift and is an excuse to show off lacy insertion stitches.

Make the wider insertion (Coin Eyelet, page 100) first, with an even number of eyelet holes to slot the ribbon through—there are 24 in this one. Join the ends of this insertion to make a ring and make two more rings of the same size with the two narrower insertions (Single Faggot Stitch, page 100). This gives the depth of the cushion. Make the cover by sewing together two rectangles of linen, leaving a section open at one end. Turn it through to the right side and sew on the insertions. Fill the cushion with stuffing and lavender heads then stitch the opening closed. Slot the ribbon through the trim and tie a bow.

PROJECT 3: SUMMER HAT

Transform an old denim hat with a fancy band and complete the look with an oversized flower.

Rickrack braid (page 73) has been used to make a striking lime-green hatband. It is necessary to knit a short length first in order to gauge the number of pattern repeats needed to fit around the hat. This measurement is fairly flexible as knitting can, within reason, be stretched or eased in according to need. The band is secured with a tiny stitch near each point of the pattern. The pinned-on flower is a Marguerite (page 109), made in a chunky yarn for a bold effect.

PROJECT 4: FLORAL BAG

A posy of knitted roses adds floral fantasy to a small fabric handbag. Alternatively, the roses could nestle at a neckline or encircle a ponytail.

The largest flower is based on Rose (page 106), with the first four petals knitted in a deeper shade of pink. The smaller flowers are similar, but omit the last three large petals. The leaves are Rose Leaf (page 105) and the three stems are made from lengths of the round knitted cord described in the Refresher Course (page 13). This is a fabric bag and so the flowers were stitched to the side. On a firmer material they could simply be glued in place.

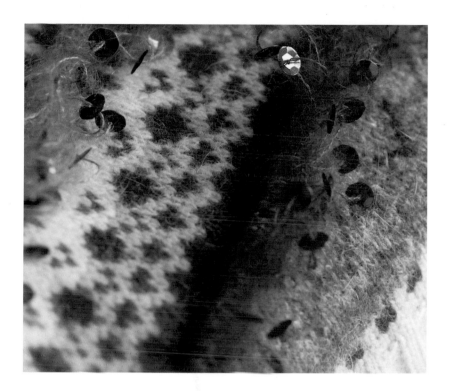

PROJECT 5: WINTER WARMERS

Plain woolen gloves clearly offer scope for embellishment, but even a patterned scarf can be enhanced with a trim.

The appliqué hearts on the gloves are simple lengths of Picot Point (page 57) curved into shape and caught down with matching sewing thread. Each heart is made up of 25 picots. The ends meet at the base with one extending below the other to make a point. A pompom (page 12) completes the motif.

Several stripes at each end of the scarf have the addition of Loops and Sequins (page 97). Each trim was laid flat and backstitched along the plain edge with matching sewing thread. The trim was then turned over and caught down to form a neat folded edge, leaving the loops free.

INDEX

RESOURCES

Websites
In addition to the sites listed below, many other yarn suppliers and useful information about yarn and knitting can be found on the internet. These are just a few websites:

www.coatsandclark.com
www.knitrowan.com
www.knitting.about.com
www.theyarnco.com
www.uniquekolours.com
www.yarnsinternational.com

Magazines
Of the many magazines of knitting designs three in particular have features on technique:

VOGUE knitting
www.vogueknitting.com

Interweave Knits Magazine
www.interweaveknits.com

Knitter's Magazine
www.knittinguniverse.com

Books
These classic reference books are mostly out of print but are worth finding:

Mary Thomas's Book of Knitting Patterns (Hodder & Stoughton) *A Treasury of Knitting Patterns, A Second Treasury of Knitting Patterns*, and *Charted Knitting Patterns* by Barbara Walker (Scribners)

The Handknitter's Handbook by Montse Stanley (David & Charles)

Dover Books
www.doverpublications.com reprint old knitting books of various types.
www.unicornbooks.com is a source of recent publications.

CREDITS

The author would like to thank Hilary Underwood for so much knitting and Susan Horan for checking the instructions.

Thanks to the following suppliers for yarns used in this book:

Debbie Bliss
Knitting Fever Inc
315 Bayview Avenue
Amityville
New York 11701
tel: 001 516 546 3600
fax: 001 516 546 6871
email: admin@knittingfever.com
web: www.knittingfever.com

Rowan and Jaeger Yarns
Distributor
Rowan c/o Westminster Fibers
165 Ledge Street
Nashua NH 03063
www.westminsterfibers.com

Jamieson & Smith
Shetland Wool Brokers Ltd
90 North Road
Lerwick ZE1 0PQ
Shetland Islands, UK
email: sales@shetlandwool.org
web: www.shetlandwool.org;
www.shetlandwoolbrokers.co.uk

Sirdar
Knitting Fever Inc
315 Bayview Avenue
Amityville
New York 11701
tel: 001 516 546 3600
fax: 001 516 546 6871
email: admin@knittingfever.com
web: www.knittingfever.com